LEARNING A TRADE

1944-1949
SECOND EDITION

A view of the eastern half of the Newport Railway workshops

GORDON J R SMITH

The drawing on the front cover is by Robert Emerson Curtis

Courtesy Arthur Spartalis Fine Art Subiaco

LEARNING A TRADE

1944-1949

SECOND EDITION

Written and produced by the author Gordon J R Smith

Copyright © Gordon J R Smith 2025

No part of this book and its contents may be reproduced for commercial publication in any form without permission in writing from the author or a member of his family.

ISBN: 978-1-7638368-2-2
National Library of Australia Cataloguing-in-Publication entry
Creator: Gordon JR Smith
Title: Learning a Trade 1944-1949 (2nd Edition)

Cover design by Gordon Smith

Tale Publishing
Melbourne Victoria

Tale

REFERENCE SOURCES

Special thanks to all of the following for the use of their work:

Victorian Railways News Letter Century Number September 1944 *(VRNLCN)*

Behind The Railway Scene Victorian Railways *(VRBTRC)*

Century Edition Power Parade Victorian Railways *(VRCEPP)*

Australian Tools Ken Arnold

Australian Railway Historical Society *(AHRS)*

Downer EDI for permission to take photos at the Newport Workshops

Arthur Spartalis of Fine Art of Subiaco W.A. for permission to use drawings of Robert Emerson Curtis, from his book *NATIONS AT WORK* some of which are reproduced.

Various images from VR historic publications I have in my possession containing no copyright restrictions.

CHAPTER INDEX

FOREWARD

1	A NEW RAIL FAN AND OUR FAMILY 1927-1937	6
2	VFL FOOTBALL THE SPIRIT AND CABLE TRAMS 1937	11
3	PRIMARY SCHOOL — THE SPIRIT AND A BUGLE 1933-1938	19
4	PRESTON TECH — A BIKE AND SCHOOL SPORTS	26
5	A NEW TECH AND MODEL RAILWAYS 1942	45
6	A Z VAN AND APPLYING FOR A JOB IN THE VR 1943	65
7	MY YEAR 1 APPRENTICESHIP BEGINS 1944-1949	69
8	THE WAR — THE GARRATT AND TWO COLLEGES 1944	86
9	THE GARRATT AND THE CUBE 1944	99
10	THE CALL UP — A BIG DECISION AND THE WAR 1944	112
11	THE CUBE IS FINALLY COMPLETE 1944	122
12	YEAR 2 APPRENTICESHIP — THE TUG AND GARRATTS 1945	128
13	VE DAY 1945 — THE TUG AND AXLE BOXES 1945	135
14	ATOM BOMB ENDS WAR — VR WAR EFFORT — THE ALPS 1945	141
15	YEAR 3 APPRENTICESHIP — BRAKES — EASTER AND SKIS 1946	152
16	THE TURNERY — COLLEGE AND TO THE SNOW 1946	162
17	A RAIL STRIKE — J J BROWN AND A BIKE TOUR 1946	169
18	A GEAR WHEEL — THE STRIKE ENDS AND MR. RICH 1946	175
19	LEARNING TO OPERATE A GRINDING MACHINE 1946	182
20	AN OXY-ACETYLENE CLASS AND COLLEGE ENDS 1946	186

21	ANNUAL LEAVE A NINE DAY HIKE IN THE ALPS 1947	193
22	THE DRAWING OFFICE – EDITHVALE AND RAIL STRIKE 1947	202
23	SKIING WITH THE ROVER SCOUTS 1947	208
24	THE 40 HOUR WEEK IS DECLARED AND AN X CLASS 1947	211
25	TO JOLIMONT WORKSHOPS AND ELECTRIC TRAINS 1947	218
26	YEAR 5 APPRENTICESHIP AND 40HR WEEK BEGIN 1948	222
27	BACK TO NEWPORT – THEN OFF TO SKI ON THE BHP 1948	226
28	I JOIN YHA – DISAPPOINTING NEWS AND SIGHTS 1948	231
29	SERVING THE EXTRA 38 DAYS TO BE A TRADESMAN 1949	238
30	I QUAFILY TO BE A TRADESMAN FITTER AND TURNER	240
	AFTERWARDS	242
	ABOUT THE AUTHOR	244

FOREWORD

Learning a Trade is a book describing my early childhood and my love of trains that eventually led me years later, to become an apprentice fitter and turner with the Victorian Railways (VR). I was born on 19th May 1927, and began my primary schooling at the Heidelberg State School. From there, because my love of trains indicated that I had a mechanical and not an analytical bent, I enrolled in a three year technical school course at the Preston Technical School, just as World War 2 was beginning. This further enhanced my interest all things mechanical, and after three enjoyable years at Preston Technical School, I left with a Senior Technical Certificate.

I then enrolled in a three year Mechanical Engineering Certificate Course at the Royal Melbourne Technical College (RMTC), but found it hard going and dropped out. With my love of railways still undiminished, I decided to take on a fitting and turning apprenticeship with the Victorian Railways, which as it turned out could not have been a better choice for my future. The five years of my apprenticeship from 1944 to 1949 at the Newport Workshops were no ordinary years. WW 2 was in a critical stage and the workshops were manufacturing a large range of war equipment. One of these was a Garratt locomotive being built at Newport as part of the war effort, on which I worked on the first day of my apprenticeship and to its completion. I also worked on a 75 foot, ocean going tug being built for the war effort.

Coupled with the story of my apprenticeship and integral to that, I have written about aspects of the life style of Victorians during those war years 1944 to 1945. Then immediately after the war in 1945 the fight by the Communist led unions for the 40 hour week began, for which the decisions to strike were largely taken at mass meetings of workers at the Newport Workshops. This resulted in many strikes during which the railway system was shut down. As an apprentice I was not on strike, but I could not get to work from my home in Rosanna. The result being that I had to make up an extra 38 days to complete my apprenticeship, extending my time into 1949, when finally I became a tradesman.

Although the war and the strikes interrupted my apprenticeship: through them I gained valuable lessons in politics, human relations and newspaper reporting. From my memory bank I have described the various training activities that I undertook during my apprenticeship. The 'jewel in the crown' of VR apprentice training was undoubtable the Victorian Railway Technical College situated adjacent to the workshops. All VR apprentices attended College for the first three years of their apprenticeship, where they were instructed in a wide range of theoretical, semi-technical and practical subjects, most of which complimented the hands on training they received in the workshops. I enjoyed my three years at the College although I did not win any of the scholarships that were offered.

Apprentice training in the VR was conducted in an extremely professional manner by the VR Apprenticeship Board under the leadership of the Apprentice Master Mr. Curtis. I believe that the training given to Victorian Railway apprentices must certainly have been the best in Victoria, if not Australia. During the five years of my apprenticeship my weekends, holidays and annual leave were very exciting and adventurous times for me with in the Rover Scouts, especially hiking and skiing, and I felt that they were a very important adjunct to my apprenticeship, because I learned a number of extra skills besides turning and fitting, learning to ski and some carpentry skills in order to make a pair of skis. I fully expected that when I became a tradesman my lifetime career would be with the VR, however that wasn't to be as reference to *About Gordon Smith,* will show at the end of this book.

It was very exciting being an apprentice specially when working on the Garratts and S class *Spirit of Progress* locomotives came in for maintenance from time to time and I was able to have a close up knowledge of the work being carried out on them. However, during my five year apprenticeship, working close by the *Spirit* locomotives I was able to observe the careful manner in which the streamlining was removed and stored, compared to the final years of my apprenticeship when the streamlining panels of these iconic, famous locomotives were sadly, uncared for.

I was saddened too, coupled with disbelief, when in later years I learned that all the S class locomotives carrying the names of Australian explorers were scrapped in 1953. This was a vicious act of corporate vandalism, which to this day has been kept secret, with only a few words about the scrappings in the very good publication titled *Spirit of Progress* by the Australian Historical Railway Society. The bright side of this for me is that I was up close and personal to the *Spirit* locomotives during some of the last years of their lives.

Most of the photos in this book of the Newport Workshops and locomotives come from three Victorian Railway booklets which I have in my possession from the *Century of the VR* in 1954, (See References Sources.) The other images; I have taken with a Baby Brownie camera with only eight exposures to a roll of film.

CHAPTER 1

A NEW RAIL FAN AND OUR FAMILY 1927-1937

"Daddy, daddy! It's a train, I can hear its whistle. Quick come and lift me up so I can see it please." My father rushed out to the back verandah, picked me up and with great glee, I was just able to see the locomotive's black chimney belching smoke and a few of the high goods wagons as they passed by on their way up the line towards Eltham and Hurstbridge. On looking back I think it would have been a Y class locomotive with its high chimney and short wheelbase. My father was born in 1900 and in 1915 joined the fire protection engineer's firm of Wormald Brothers, as an office boy. In 1929 after becoming a bookkeeper he was made redundant when Wormalds moved some of their offices to Sydney. This was the time of the beginning of the great depression. I was not aware of this and never questioned why he was not at work.

The author's parents and the author before he was aware of the existence of trains

I kept my ears pricked as I waited for the sound of the whistle from the goods train when it returned and passed through Rosanna on its way back to Melbourne. Once my father heard the whistle he would hurry out and lift me up again in time for me to see the train, and that would make a very exciting day for me. I believe the year was 1931, and I would have been four years old having been born on 19th May 1927. My mother was pregnant with her second child, a boy, born on 5th October 1932. He was named Donald. Soon my father found work, which was a great relief for my mother, especially because she now had a new baby to look after.

I did not have a father to lift me up when I heard a train coming, but I had grown a little taller and whenever I heard the exciting sound of a locomotive's chime whistle, I could see the engine and some of the goods wagons by standing on a sturdy wooden butter box. Sometimes I was allowed to run out to the street in front of our house at 16 Hillside Road, where there were no houses to block my view and hardly any cars to worry about, so I was always thrilled to be able to see the complete locomotive and goods wagons as they passed by at the bottom of the road.

My baby brother Donald was wheeled around in our new big pram with large, but thin spoked wheels and this opened up a new exciting contact with trains. Every now and again I would go with my mother and Donald in the pram down to the Rosanna station, where we would catch the train that only ran once each hour to visit my mother's mother in Ivanhoe, a few stations on the way to Melbourne. With the help of the guard we lifted the pram into the quite large guard's compartment. I chose to sit on the long bench seat directly in front of the driver's cabin and through the driver's window I watched with complete fascination, as the overhead catenary wires weaved a pattern from side to side during the journey. Sometimes at the stations in between, we were joined by other mothers with babies in prams and with young children at their side and this provided great enjoyment too. It was great fun also to be with the guard and see him blow his whistle and raise his green flag as the signal for the driver to begin moving the train to the next station. These exciting sights were repeated again on the way back home from our visit to my grandmother. I had another grandmother, my father's mother and she lived in Greensborough, a couple of stations further up the line from Rosanna.

The author and grandpa Griffin

To differentiate between the two, my mother's mother lived in Ivanhoe, so we called her 'Ivanhoe Gram', and my father's mother we called 'Greensborough Gram' because she lived in Greensborough. After Ivanhoe Gram's husband died many years ago, Ivanhoe Gram lived with her sister in law who we called Auntie Barbara, a nice, kind old lady. Every now and again we would catch the train to visit Greensborough Gram, and this usually happened on a weekend, which meant that my father was always with us. On these visits we never travelled in the guard's van, because my father would help us lift the big pram into a carriage compartment

Ivanhoe Gram

through the narrow swing door. Greensborough Gram lived about ten minutes' walk from the station, and after I had played with Melva, Greensborough Gram's daughter about the same age as me, we would be called in for the evening meal. By this time it was nearly dark and Greensborough Gram's house didn't have electricity. I will

Greensborough gram

never forget the sight of the big dining room table with all the plates and cutlery laid out neatly. In the centre of the table there was a small, bright candle in a lovely decorated candle holder, encircled by a tall, curved glass cover. It wasn't a candle I soon discovered, but a beautiful kerosene lamp that emitted a lovely, pleasant woody smell. Greensborough Gram's husband Mr. Griffin (grandpa) was still alive. He was a kindly old gentleman with an elegant, white beard and he sat at the head of the table.

It was a really magical dinner eating by the light of the lamp although it was not as easy to see the food as with an electric light, which seemed strange to me at the time, because we had travelled to Greensborough in an electric train, which looking back was quite good logic or my age. We visited Greensborough Gram many times after that first time, but I cannot ever remember being there when the house had been wired for power. Not long after dinner we left and walked in the dark down to the Greensborough station. We did not have long to wait before the bright light of the train appeared in the distance. As it drew nearer and nearer, I got a fright because it appeared to be heading straight for the end of the platform, only to take a sharp turn at the last moment and pull in to the station. We climbed aboard with the pram and I got to the open window.

When I looked out, I smelt the pleasant odour of burning kerosene again, this time wafting along the platform from the porter's kerosene lamp as he held it high to show a green light to the guard and shouted "All clear". When the guard was sure that all the passengers were safely aboard, and that all the doors were closed he blew his whistle and held his lamp up high, showing the driver a green signal to let the driver know it was safe to start the train. I was not only enthralled to observe all these sights, sounds and smells, but I was also learning a little about the Victorian Railway's (VR) safe working. Trains, one of the loves of my life, was largely fashioned by those early childhood experiences.

CHAPTER 2

VFL FOOTBALL THE SPIRIT AND CABLE TRAMS 1937

My father was a very devoted supporter of the Essendon football team, which he began following when he lived in Richmond as a young boy. Essendon in those years played on a ground, which eventually became part of the site of the Jolimont rail yards. My mother too, was an enthusiastic supporter of Essendon by marriage, and of course I was as well, by birth. My recollection of the first time I went to a football match, was one Saturday morning in the winter footy season, when my mother put Donald in the big pram and off we went by train, with the pram in the guard's compartment to Ivanhoe Gram's place at 44 Abbotsford Grove Ivanhoe. We had lunch there, usually succulent grilled barracuda, which required careful, but juicy eating so that you didn't swallow a bone. After lunch we left Donald now two years old, with Ivanhoe Gram and my mother took me by the hand and we walked nearly a mile to the Darebin railway station.

My father by this time had managed to get a job with S. A. Cheney Motors in Melbourne and he worked on Saturday mornings. My mother and I caught the train to Princes Bridge and I was surprised when suddenly the lights in the carriage were turned on. Then looking through the window all I could see was darkness punctuated by twinkling lights going past, because this was my first experience of travelling through the Richmond tunnels. Before the only tunnel I had been through in the train, was the short tunnel between Rosanna and Heidelberg stations and the carriage lights were never turned on for that tunnel.

When we arrived at Princess Bridge we changed there for the train to take us to Essendon. It was an exciting journey as I saw many types of locomotives in the North Melbourne yards, particularly E and Y classes, the most locomotives type that were to be seen in those locations at the time. The train's carriages that we travelled into Essendon were quite different to the carriages on our line. These carriages had sliding doors and I didn't like them because I couldn't open the windows adjacent to the sliding doors. The seating arrangement was different too, and nowhere near as comfortable as the trains on our line. We eventually arrived at the large Essendon railway station and walked up Napier Street to the Essendon football ground, a big football oval with a large, wooden, grandstand overlooking the oval. My mother led me up a series of steps and we sat down on one of the rows of long, wooden, bench seats waiting for my father to arrive, which very soon he did.

The Essendon grandstand later named the R S Reynold's stand

There was a game of baseball being played and a big net behind the batter's box protecting the main scoreboard from fly balls mishit by the batsman. A baseball game was the curtain raiser to many Victorian Football League (VFL) football games in those years. Our seat gave us a great view of the ground and the Dandenong Ranges in the distance, with the brick building of the Essendon High School rising just behind the ground. While we were waiting for the game to start, I had a look at my father's *Football Record,* 'The Footy Record' for short, a small booklet that listed all the players names and numbers, as well as other items of football interest. It also had provision to record with a pencil the statistics of the game as it was played. More to the point of my interest I heard the thrilling sound of a locomotive chime whistle, and I quickly left my seat and hurried to the side of the grandstand, but I only saw the funnel belching smoke and steam and some of the top part of a big locomotive and the roofs of the carriages as it passed by. However it was quite a thrill.

At last the players ran out on the ground, Essendon in red and black, but I have no memory of the team we played that day. There was one very famous footballer playing for Essendon at the time, the captain 'Dicky' Reynolds, and he was definitely the favourite player of the Essendon supporters who cheered loudly every time he got the ball. We all barracked madly during the game and there was too much noise to be able to hear a locomotive whistle. The game of football going on was what absorbed all of my interest until half time when I saw another locomotive and train passing by. This time I climbed up higher on the grandstand stairs and got a much better view of the big, black locomotive and the carriages as it sped by. My father said it was probably going to Seymour.

At the end of the game, which I think Essendon must have won, because both my father and mother were very happy. They helped me roll up a number of discarded footy records and tie them together with a piece of string that my father always carried for the purpose. We left the grandstand and walked out on to the centre of the ground where I kicked the make believe football around while my father with pencil in hand studied the scoreboard, and using a letter code in the footy record, wrote down the results of the other games that were played that Saturday as they were posted on the scoreboard. By now it was getting dark and my father had got all the results noted down, so we made our way down Napier Street to the railway station.

On the way back in the train to Flinders Street I kept a lookout from a window to see what trains I could see. One that was very exciting was when a steam hauled passenger train passed by, and I saw a dimly lit series of blurred rectangular lights from the carriage windows and some much brighter lights from larger windows as the dining car of the train quickly sped by. Finally our train reached Flinders Street where we crossed to number one platform by the subway. A passenger train was standing there and passengers were boarding the train, which my father said was due to leave for Sale and Bairnsdale in about five minutes. There were a few trolleys on the platform loaded with large metal canisters. The porters were very busy unloading them and with a big thump sliding them on to the floor of each passenger compartment. "What are those things for?" I asked my father; "Foot warmers." He said.

We walked along the train until we came to the front carriage, in front of which a large, black locomotive was making a series of strange noises. This was the closest I had ever been to a steam locomotive, and this one was very big, much larger than the ones I had seen in the distance from my front verandah or the road. My mother kept her distance from the engine, but my father took me by the hand and we walked up close alongside it. I must admit I was a little frightened by the noises coming from this huge, black engine and the wisps of steam coming from various locations around its black boiler and large wheels. Some of the noises coming from the locomotive were quite weird, a steady pant and an eerie whine were the most predominant. Neither of these sounds were unpleasant, in fact they became a couple of the sounds that I loved to hear coming from steam locomotives. I was to learn later that the panting was produced by the locomotive's steam driven air compressor that provided compressed air for the Westinghouse brakes and other uses, and the high pitched whine came from the steam driven turbo generator that provided electricity for the locomotive's large headlight and cab lights. With my father holding my hand I cautiously moved close to the cab and was able to catch a glimpse of the fire and feel its heat, when the firebox door was opened for the fireman to quickly shovel some coal into the glowing, red, furnace. I looked up in admiration at the driver clad in blue overalls and peaked, blue, cloth cap, topped with a pair of goggles, but he failed to acknowledge our presence. It was evident that the train was about to leave as there were green flags being raised and whistles being blown, so my father slowly led me back away from the side of the locomotive. Suddenly as I watched, the driver pulled the whistle cord and I nearly fell backwards as the chime whistle sounded very loudly, a sound I was to grow to love throughout all the years of my life. I watched entranced as a noisy cloud of steam came from the front of the locomotive and a low level puff of steam and smoke came from the chimney as very slowly with a few more stronger puffs, the locomotive and train gathered speed and soon the whole train was gone with only a red and white light showing on the back of the guard's van.

Then it was up the ramp and in to a not so exciting electric train to Ivanhoe to have tea with Ivanhoe Gram, before with my mother and father I helped push the pram to the Ivanhoe station for the journey home, after a great day of watching my first game of football, and being up close to a huge locomotive, watching spellbound and a little frightened, as it changed from being a huge, black, fire breathing, stationary object, to one of immense moving power, were two of the most thrilling events of my young life. My father told me later that the locomotive we saw was an A^2 class.

Going to Essendon to watch a football match with my parents for the first time was the beginning of many more trips to the ground to watch Essendon play and I soon became a very knowledgeable supporter of the team, which at that time were not called *The Bombers*, but *The Dons* amongst other names. Believe it or not one of the other names was the *Blood Stained Niggers*. Of course Essendon were also called many unflattering names by our opponents. After the first time I went to the Essendon football ground I also went to many other football grounds to watch Essendon play other teams, Footscray, Fitzroy, Collingwood and North Melbourne to name a few.

Footscray and Collingwood were my favourites, particularly Footscray because the sounds of locomotive whistles were to be heard for most of the game and even sometimes over the noise of the cheering. Before the game and at half time I spent much of those periods up on the embankment watching trains go by. Leaving the Footscray ground after the game one afternoon we crossed the footbridge over the railway tracks, and I well remember a beautiful, tantalising, sight that met my eyes. The sun was just about to drop below the horizon and a number of long lines of polished, bright bronze, rails stretched away in the distance to the west towards the setting sun. Where did they lead to I wondered. What was out there over the horizon? It was going to be some years before I learnt the answer to that question.

For many of my young winter years this was to be my main interest each Saturday. These journeys to Essendon and other grounds gave me the opportunity to see and learn a lot about the railways on lines other than the Rosanna line, and also to be able to see many different types of VR locomotives. I quickly began to be able to recognise many locomotive classes A^2, X, N and C classes, which were the most prevalent as we travelled through North Melbourne yards, not to forget of course the hard working dirty Y and E class. My favourite at that time was the X class, which toward the end of the winter when it was not quite dark, I always saw one of these magnificent, powerful locomotives simmering away at the head of a long goods train, just outside Spencer Street station waiting to get the signal to begin its journey, which I think looking back, by the direction it was facing to somewhere in Gippsland.

There was another journey on rails introduced to me by my dear old Ivanhoe Gram that I was to enjoy immensely. During the years 1855 to 1940 Melbourne had more than a dozen cable tram routes radiating from its centre. It was in fact one of the largest cable tram systems in the world. To enjoy the delights of this mode of transport, Ivanhoe Gram would take me from my home in Rosanna by yellow bus to Ivanhoe and along Darebin Street to High Street Northcote, where we boarded a cable tram. Not to sit-mind you-in the closed trailer or saloon car as it was also called, but to sit on the very front open seats of the dummy or 'grip car.'

A cable tram trailer and grip car

In the centre of the dummy the 'grip man' stood operating a long lever, which gripped the cable running beneath the road to propel the cable tram forwards. Besides the grip lever there was also a smaller lever used to operate the brakes. There we sat with the rails disappearing just beneath our seat, an exhilarating and new experience for me of riding the rails. The cable tram took us through Clifton Hill, and then along Smith Street Collingwood, until the cable tram eventually ran down Bourke Street to Swanston Street where we got off. I had never imagined that I would experience such a wonderful open air ride on rails, so much more spine-tingling than riding in the guard's compartment of a train with my mother.

Ivanhoe Gram then took me to the Robur Tea Rooms in Swanston Street where we had scrumptious, brown bread rolls, with butter and cheese. After exploring many of the shops we caught the tram again in Bourke Street. It was more difficult to get the front seats on the dummy because there were more people wanting to ride on the tram from the city than was the case in Northcote, so we had to be to be content to ride in the less exciting, closed trailer car.

Back home in the yellow bus ended a fabulous day on rails. There were some places on the system such as where cable trams changed between double tracks by means of crossover rails, where the trams had to be pushed as there was no cable running under the crossover. There were other such locations where this was also required. The Northcote cable tram route was one of the last and was replaced by London style, red double-decker buses, which operated for some years, but riding in the front seats of the top deck was no match for the front seats of the dummy of a cable tram.

CHAPTER 3

PRIMARY SCHOOL *THE SPIRIT* AND BUGLE 1933-1938

In 1933 I began school at the Heidelberg State School 294 and I was very happy there. This school I believe was unique in that it had its own swimming pool in which I swam during the five years I was at the school. It was quite a big concrete pool, but it was not chlorinated. I never contracted any medical problem however that I could have blamed on the water in the pool, although I swallowed mouthfuls of pool water from time to time and peed in the pool as I suppose most everyone else did. When we were told to bring our togs as we would be allowed in the pool the next day, a wave of anticipated excitement would pass through the classroom.

Heidelberg State School 294

As well as swimming in the school pool, building bonfires with the help of my parents and other children and their parents, was another delight that thrilled me in those early school years. We built bonfires twice each year. On Guy Fawkes Day 5th November and on Empire Day 25th May. The bonfires were quite large as there was no shortage of fuel, like spare wood and other materials around in those days. Our bonfires were built on the paddock just up from our house and when it was dark on the appointed dates, one of the parents lit the bonfire amid many exclamations of wonder and joy. Prior to the night we had all been given some pocket money and we went to the newsagent where we bought a range of fire crackers, Catherine wheels, double bungers, jumping Jacks, Tom thumbs and best of all sky rockets. As the flames and sparks rose in the night air the fun began as we all lit up our fire crackers amid squeals and shouts of delight. Our parents were the only ones allowed to set off the sky rockets that were propped up in milk bottles ready to light. These were always the last to be lit producing great yells of admiration and awe as they lit up the night sky in vivid patterns of light. As well as our bonfire, other bonfires could be seen dotted around the many hills surrounding Rosanna. I feel sorry for the young people and parents who nowadays can no longer enjoy some of these pleasures that were an integral part of growing up as young children as we did.

One of our school teachers Mr. Probert was a retired army bugler and he taught those of us who could afford to buy a bugle to play it. I was one of those lucky ones and was thrilled to be able to buy a bugle and begin learning to play the instrument. It took quite some time before me and the other students mastered the art of pursing our lips, together with a bit of spitting, before we were able to play the Last Post and Reveille. On Anzac Day our school, led by those of us who had learned to play the bugle and a few students with drums, marched up Burgundy Street to the war memorial. This was a wonderful

Our band on Anzac Day at the Memorial
The author is in the back row nearest the camera

experience that made the sometimes frustrating task of learning to play the bugle all worthwhile. Those of us who were in the Scouts were asked to wear our uniforms, which added to the enjoyment of the event. During the five years of learning at the Heidelberg State School I had many friends, especially a tall kid called Harry Gilham who became a lifelong friend. He joined the Cubs with me and we both graduated into the 1st Heidelberg Scouts together, where I met another lifelong friend Roy Quilliam. We used to meet regularly, but sadly as I write Harry and Roy have left this earth.

In 1937 I was in the fifth grade, and there was some news about that the Victorian Railways (VR) was building a new modern train called the *Spirit of Progress*. The train was being built to replace the Albury Express that sometimes required the use of two A^2 locomotives to haul the train of wooden carriages carrying passengers on the Melbourne to Albury railway line. On arrival at Albury the passengers, because of the break of gauge, had to change into a NSW train to take them on to Sydney. Coming from the football this was the train that I saw sometimes and marvelled at as it sped by my window. The new train was to be composed of all steel carriages and be hauled by only one streamlined, three cylinder, S class locomotive more powerful and faster than the A^2 class locomotives.

Sometime after the end of the 1937 football season my father showed me the local newspaper that was running a competition open to anyone of school age. The competition was to make a coloured drawing of the new train's locomotive, of which there was an outline given in the paper. The prize was a six month pass to the Saturday matinee at *The Orient,* Heidelberg's new oriental styled movie theatre. My father said I should enter, so I said I would. He helped me collect coloured publicity brochures of the train and locomotive, and I set to work making my drawing with crayons. Subsequently just prior to the *Spirit of Progress* being unveiled the results were announced in the local paper. I had won! The tickets for Saturday's matinees were for the summer months, so did not clash with going to the football. Every Saturday afternoon would see me walk a mile from my home to the theatre, stand up for the playing of God Save the King, then enjoy a serial about aeroplanes and some shorts. It was a truly wonderful experience for me. On the black and white screen I saw newsreels of events around the world (mainly at the time concerning Hitler), cowboy movies starring Hoppalong Cassidy, and once a movie the name of which, I have never forgotten, *Tell Me Tonight,* starring Richard Crooks a famous tenor.

The complete new streamlined train the *Spirit of Progress* was built in the Newport Workshops and became an icon of the VR. The locomotive was functionally, but beautifully streamlined with a sloping front, which carried a winged, gold emblem of the VR at its centre below the large headlight. The complete train from the front of the locomotive to the observation car at the end of the train was painted in royal blue with two gold stripes that were continued along whole length of the train, producing a stunning and beautiful visual effect of speed and elegance. It was said that the locomotive was streamlined in the art deco style, but I am quite familiar with this art form and this was not so, although many of the publicity posters on display were certainly in the art deco style. Of interest however, the locomotive that hauled the 20th Century Limited passenger train of the New York Central System in America is a very good example of excellent art deco styling applied to a locomotive.

The Spirit of Progress

The *Spirit of Progress* hereafter referred to as '*The Spirit*' was hauled by one of the four streamlined S class three cylinder 'Pacific' type locomotives. Each of these streamlined locomotives was given the names of an Australian Pioneer explorer. S 300, Mathew Flinders, S 301, Sir Thomas Mitchell, S 302 Edward Henty and S 303 C J Latrobe. The train consisted of twelve air conditioned carriages, one of which was a dining car and the last one a parlour or observation car, as it would be described in America and I also like to call it, being more descriptive of the outward appearance of the last car of the train. Directly behind the tender was a bulk mail van. All the carriages were made of welded Cor-Ten (Corten) steel. After a few trial runs to Geelong on the 23rd November 1937 amid much celebration, *The Spirit* left Spencer Street Station at 6.30 p.m. for its inaugural journey to Albury arriving there at the scheduled time of 10.20 p.m.

Three of the four S class locomotives as they looked prior to streamlining

Once on the way to the football I was thrilled to see in the North Melbourne yards, one of *The Spirit's* locomotives resplendent in its blue and gold striped livery and I yelled out in delight: "Quick look there's The *Spirit of Progress!*" Whatever the result of the Essendon match was that day, win or lose, I cannot remember which, but seeing *The Spirit* locomotive made my day. For many years *The Spirit* sped to Albury and return carrying an average of 400 first and second class passengers each way in air conditioned luxury. Sometimes coming home in the train after the football at Essendon, *The Spirit* passed by in a flash of blue and brightly lit windows, depending how light it was. However, it was always something to eagerly look forward to after the football, when the match was played at Essendon.

It was not only *The Spirit* that came on the scene in 1937, but our family gained another son Geoffrey, born on the 2nd March. Donald, the new born Geoff and I were spaced at five year intervals. I knew my father was a methodical man and after working in various jobs leading up to 1940, he became a certified accountant and by 1942, he had secured a position as an Office Manager with Cox Brothers in Bourke Street Melbourne a large, clothing, manchester and furniture business. My father had a staff of 36 females, lucky father. He had certainly come a long way since the time when out of work, he lifted me up on the verandah, to watch the goods trains go by. My father worked at Cox Brothers on Saturday mornings, and in the winter football season, I would meet him there and hurry off to catch the train at Flinders Street to take us to the football. My brother Geoff told me many years later before my mother died in 1990 (my father had already passed away in 1982) that he plucked up enough courage to ask my mother about the regular, five year spacing of their three children? "I left that to your father." My mother replied.

I completed my primary school education in 1938 at the Heidelberg State School and received my Merit Certificate. The next step in my education had to be decided upon. Because I had shown a definite interest in mechanical objects, railways for one, it was decided that I should go to a technical school and not a high school. The closest technical school was Collingwood, to which I could have gone by train, but it was thought by my parents that Preston would be the better technical school for me. I wondered if this choice was influenced in any way by the fact that we barracked for Essendon and the Collingwood football team was, shall I say, not too popular with Essendon supporters, in fact we hated them.

I applied to join the Preston Technical School and found that I would have to sit for an entrance examination. On the day of the exam my mother and I walked a mile to the bus stop alongside the Heidelberg Cemetery where we caught a red bus, which took us some four miles along Bell Street, to the Preston Technical School in St. Georges Road just off Bell Street Preston. The Preston Technical School was a large, two storey, L shaped, cream, brick building. Contained in the legs of the L there was a large bitumen quadrangle. It was quite an impressive school and I hoped to become one of its students. We were told when we signed in that the exam would only take about an hour so my mother elected to wait. As soon as the exam was finished off we went back home. On the way my mother asked me. "What was the exam like? Did I think I passed?' "It was pretty easy and I reckon I'll pass." I replied. Sure enough a short time later I was notified that I had passed and was enrolled for the 'Class of 1939.'

The Preston Technical school in 1939 in St. Georges Road Preston
Photo NMIT

CHAPTER 4
PRESTON TECH-A BIKE AND SCHOOL SPORTS 1939-1941

My family bought me a beaut *Malvern Star* bike for Christmas, a 28 inch (70 cm) diameter wheel the standard size at the time. The *Malvern Star* bike was made famous by Sir Hubert Opperman an Australian cyclist who won many Australian bike races as well as many in Europe on this brand of bike. Until the time when I began school at the Preston Technical School, which from hereon I will refer to as 'The Tech', I practised riding on my new bike and after many long and short rides on various roads, I was quite sure of myself and my bike riding ability.

The author with his Malvern Star bike

My father asked me; "Gordon, do you feel that you could ride your bike there and back to Preston each day instead of going by the bus?" Without a moment's hesitation I said firmly; "I am sure I could." So it was settled. I decided however, to do a trial ride there and back, which I accomplished that without any trouble. I had a milometer attached to one of the bike forks, which was operated by a peg attached to a spoke. The journey I found took me just over 30 minutes each way, and my milometer showed me that the distance there and back was 8.4 miles (13.4 km). Afterwards my father said he was pleased that I had done the ride, and he had no qualms about me riding my bike to school.

As well as going to a new school I also passed up from the Cubs to the 1st Heidelberg Scout troop, which was a very pleasing move. However, my first night at the Scouts was not at all pleasing, although only in one respect. We played a game of 'blind man's boxing' in which the opponents donned boxing gloves and were blindfolded. We boxed away at each other amid yells from the onlookers encouraging us on. My opponent Ian Howard was probably the tallest scout in our troop and I was the shortest. Ian thought he was attempting to strike me in the chest or stomach, but due to the difference in our heights he was actually aiming at my head and after quite a number of punches with many missing their mark, one of Ian's blind punches connected with my head and I went down for the count!

I could not have been knocked out by a more appropriate scout that night, because Ian at the time was studying to be a doctor at the Melbourne University. I quickly recovered thanks in part to Ian, putting in practise some of the skills he had learned at the University. So ended my first scout meeting, but of course there were many more exciting and rewarding, less traumatic scout meetings to be enjoyed over many years.

Just before I began school at The Tech, on one very hot, dark, summer night, our family and neighbours stood on the road outside our house looking toward the east to the Dandenong Ranges, where we could see the orange glow of fires burning. The date was Friday 13th January 1939, *'Black Friday,'* when bush fires wiped out a large percentage of Victoria's forests together with many lives being lost. In the years after the fires, my view of the mountains changed from blue-green to grey-white. This change produced some beautiful light and shadow effects on the mountains, especially in the afternoon light, when the sun's rays fell on the dead tree trunks, the mountains appearing as though they were covered in snow. A very tragic beauty. I learnt the names and heights in feet of every summit that I could see from the high viewpoints in Rosanna and Heidelberg and I still remember many of them to this day.

I was looking forward with great joy not only to beginning my technical school education, but riding my bike there and back each day. At last the day for the opening of The Tech came along and with a knapsack on my back containing my lunch and a pencil case; I rode the four miles to The Tech along Bell Street. Bell Street was not the busy street it is today, a divided road with shops and factories along its length, together with being a very busy, cross suburb thoroughfare. The main traffic at the time along the two, single lane street was the red bus, a spattering of cars, small trucks and an occasional horse drawn vehicle. I was quite confident that as long as I rode sensibly I would not have any problem. I knew too that I would also need to look after the maintenance of my bike diligently, keeping it cleaned and oiled, the tyres pumped up properly and the chain correctly adjusted, if I wished to ride my bike to The Tech for the three years I would be there.

The Tech's uniform that my parents bought for me was a rather colourful burgundy, blue and grey striped cap, V neck jumper and tie, but it was not compulsory to wear them, although I did with pride on many special occasions. When I began classes at The Tech I found that I enjoyed all the subjects that I had to learn. I remember Physics that consisted of sound, heat and light, Chemistry and English, and it was in the English class that I met my first foreigner, a young, fair haired Italian lad, called Lorenzo. Our teacher had Lorenzo tell us about Italy and the words of a song, the name of which I cannot recall, but I certainly can recall the words, (but not the spelling) *"Sul mar a luchiga castro del genta placida londa barketa mia."* It was fun and I remember the tune to this day. The words I discovered later were from the song called *Santa Lucia*. Harry Gilham was at The Tech at the same time as me, although we did not see much of each other there, but met at scout meetings each week and on many scout trips to various places, together with Roy.

On September 3rd 1939 war was declared with Germany, but my parents did not seem to be greatly worried. Shortly after learning of the terrible news of the declaration of war, one day at The Tech we were told that the Combined Victorian Technical School Sports (CVTSS) were to be held at Ballarat and that any student who wanted to go and book a seat on the train should let their teacher know. The (CVTSS) was an athletic competition open to any Victorian Technical School that could field a team for foot racing, jumping in its various forms and other field sports. Of course when I heard that travel there was by train I hoped I would be able to go.

I pedalled home from school that afternoon as fast as I could and told my parents all about the sports. "Can I go please go and can I have the money to get a ticket?" I asked my parents. The cost was quite cheap as I remember, and after some consideration they gave me the money. Oh, how thankful I was and my anticipation of a great train trip behind a big steam locomotive kept me in great emotional expectancy for about a month. On the 19th May I had my twelfth birthday and by then I was quite used to travelling by train by myself to the Scouts and Cubs as well as going in to the city to meet my father at Cox Brothers to go to the football with him. At last the morning of the journey came about and I caught the train from Rosanna to Spencer Street Station, where we were met by our teachers, who were each allocated a number of students to look after.

Around 9 a.m. the train pulled in to the station and we all scrambled to get a good seat by the window, especially me. I could hear, but not see the locomotive at the head of our train, however I thought it would have to be an A^2 class. Very soon with a loud whistle the train slowly pulled away from the station. I was absolutely ecstatic as I looked out the window as the train clickety-clicked through North Melbourne and the yards where I saw many more locomotives, one a tank engine a D^4 class that I had never seen before. After crossing two rivers on big steel bridges, imagine my delight when I saw we were passing through Footscray and to the right I saw the Footscray football ground. At last, not only was I going to see where those railway lines went to over the horizon towards the setting sun, I was actually travelling along those same lines. It was so wonderful to see what lay over that horizon, wayside paddocks with crops of I knew not what.

Then after stopping at a station (Bacchus Marsh) and picking up more students, our train began a long, slow climb at the top of which, I beheld a magnificent view that stretched away below the train all the way to the sunny horizon in the north. Wonderful too was hearing the puffing of the locomotive, sometimes loud and at other times hardly heard, but throughout the journey I never grew tired of hearing the stirring sound of the chime whistle of the A^2. The whistle was being blown nearly continuously at many places along the line as the driver of the A^2 warned the drivers of the few cars that there were on the roads at that time that our train was rapidly approaching a level crossing or other cause of danger. There were of course at that time, many horse drawn vehicles, drays, carts and the like that were not as agile as cars or persons to get out of the way of a speeding locomotive and train. Many household needs such as bread, milk, ice and other items were being delivered by horse and

One of the A^2 class locomotives that hauled our train

cart, including the 'night man' who collected the pans by horse and cart.

At last sometime near noon our train pulled into the large Ballarat station and under the care of our teacher we walked quite a long way to the Ballarat football ground. There were school kids everywhere some wearing uniforms. I was wearing my tech cap and jumper as were most others from The Tech. We were not the only technical school on the train; I think some Collingwood and Footscray students also travelled with us. I managed to get a quick look at the locomotive and yes, it was an A^2.

Before I went on the train to the sports, behind The Tech's quadrangle there was a grassed field and I remembered seeing students running, jumping and playing other games there, so I imagined that this was where they had trained and were selected to get a place in the sport's team. I had made friends with some kids at the school and met them on the train. At the ground we sat around eating our lunches. The games began and we watched for a while, but did not have a clue which of the students competing in the various events were from our school, or for that matter any other school, so it became quite boring.

Later in the day our teacher told us we were free to go and explore the city as long as we did not get lost and were back on the Ballarat station by 4.30 p.m. We left the games and made our way in to the big city where we bought ice creams and lollies. I had a watch and so did one of my friends, so there was no danger that we would not get back to the station by 4.30 p.m. I was surprised to find that the city of Ballarat was so big, with large buildings, many as high as some in Melbourne, and there were also many people to be seen. After wandering up and down the streets looking at all the various shops for quite a while we decided it was time to make our way back to the station, arriving there well before 4.30 p.m. The train we discovered, was due to leave at 5 p.m. so I had a good look at the locomotive, a magnificent black A^2 that was already at the head of our train, and watched many of the other engines working in the yard.

Gradually all the students collected on the platform and the teachers too, some of whom did not appear to be quite steady on their feet. Finally our teacher, who was not unsteady like some of the others collected our group of students and checked that we were all present, and just before 5 p.m. we were allowed to board the train. Luckily I managed to get a window seat with a window that opened. The carriages were of the BPL class that have sliding doors and the windows next to the sliding doors cannot be opened, because when the sliding doors are open, they open in front of the windows. On the way back I kept a lookout, watching signals. Sometimes I could see the locomotive as the train rounded sharp curves, which gave me a thrilling view of the locomotive's motion gear (connecting and coupling rods) moving up and down and around and around with steam and smoke coming from the chimney. Well before we reached Spencer Street, it gradually became dark and the signals by the side of the line were all showing green aspects as we passed by, and this too was another great sight. There was only one drawback. I kept getting bits of coal dust in my eyes and eventually as we neared Melbourne, I just sat back and enjoyed the sound and movement of the train.

Back in Spencer Street Station I found my way home and told my parents and Donald all about my wondrous journey and thanked my parents for letting me go. I now knew what was over the horizon and marvelled at what I had seen and experienced. An exhilarating and thrilling train journey through glorious scenery, but most remarkable and unexpected of all was being in the large city of Ballarat. The trip was in itself a grand geography lesson. Which tech school won the sports? I did not know, nor did anyone else I talked to from the school know. I don't think we cared. My interests during that day lay elsewhere!

I got through my first year at The Tech OK, both learning and riding the bike in summer, autumn, winter and spring without any problems, I can't remember if I was cold, hot, wet or freezing, but I imagine that I must have experienced all of those weather conditions. Such is the impervious nature of youth that they could not have been too bad, because I do not remember anything about those discomforts, except riding through the rain and sometimes hanging on to the bumper bar of the red bus, not for too far however. I had a leather motor cyclist's helmet with ear flaps and a good raincoat that kept me warm and dry on cold and wet days.

Over Christmas and New Year before my second year at The Tech began, I of course spent a lot of time with my two brothers especially Donald who was seven years old and a good brother to me. Geoff was only two years old and not yet really able to play games with us. We had about eight apricot trees that produced an abundant supply of very good apricots and I helped to pick the apricots and also to eat them. It was a wonder we never ended up looking like an apricot with apricot coloured faces, because we ate them in huge quantities.

Our Scouts on Puffing Billy's water tower

I also went on various scout outings, hiking once along the narrow gauge *Puffing Billy* railway line and was amazed to see the little locomotive looking as though it had been cut off at the knees, its small wheels nearly hidden by steam and its motion gear moving madly up and down and in and out all at once. We waved as the train went by with the little locomotive's high pitched whistle, echoing around the line side gum trees, but so unlike a chime whistle of the big locomotives.

I also went on many bike rides by myself getting to know the countryside around the hills beyond Eltham, Hurstbridge and to the Kangaroo Grounds lookout tower, from where one of the best views of the mountains and Melbourne can be seen. Leaving there was a glorious downhill ride that took me to Warrandyte on the Yarra River, and from there back home tired, but happy with the new sights that I had seen. We were not too worried by the war news, but we could not help but wonder what lay ahead.

Having successfully completed my first year at The Tech and a very happy and successful year it was, I was eager to begin my second year. I found that many aspects of learning and life at The Tech had changed from my first year; a high cyclone wire fence had been erected around the school and its large quadrangle. I never really found out the reason for this, but maybe it had something to do with the war, which by now in 1940 was also in its second year. The gates in the cyclone fence were only opened at lunchtimes and after school finished. There were new subjects to learn in my second year at The Tech, a couple of them practical subjects, Clay Modelling, and Woodwork. These together with Mathematics, Chemistry, English and Physics kept me very busy although unlike what I see today, I was not laden with a big, heavy, backbreaking, rucksack type schoolbags containing text books and homework and God knows what else.

At the end of this year I would, if I passed, earn my Junior Technical Certificate. I never really excelled in Clay Modelling, but our teacher Mr. Morrison was also teaching some of the students the game of baseball. I was very interested because I had seen the game being played as a curtain raiser when I went to the football, so I decided to learn about the game. Two of his student baseballers besides me and a couple of other boys, were two brothers Ross and

Lyn Straw. When my father heard I was interested in the game he bought me a glove and I found that baseball next to football at that time, were my two favourite sports, one for watching and one for playing.

Ross Straw became Victoria and Australia's champion baseballer. He played baseball for Essendon in the 40s and was the captain and later the coach of the Essendon Baseball Club, eventually becoming its administrator. It is quite possible that I saw Ross play in curtain raiser baseball games in later years when I went to the football at Essendon, but if he did, I did not recognise him, or heard his name mentioned. There is now in Royal Park Melbourne, a dedicated baseball oval named in his honour, the Ross Straw Field. I well remember many balls caught in my glove pitched from the strong arm of Ross Straw, each of which hurt my hand, but what a privilege it was. Ross Straw the champion baseballer, administrator, coach and Olympic champion was without doubt in my opinion, a more accomplished and award winning Australian sportsman than Don Bradman.

Mathematics was mainly Algebra and our teacher Mr. Conroy was a permanently, red faced man, with a military bearing. He took the Monday morning assembly from the brick parapet by the side of the quadrangle stairs, shouting out various commands in a high pitched, loud voice. "Attention-At Ease," I think he thought we were his army. I suspect in fact that he was a frustrated Colonel, never having risen above the rank of Captain. On 27th May 1940 the horrendous Dunkirk evacuation began, which was very bad news for the Allies and its aftermath caused a wave of gloom that spread around Australia.

One Monday morning soon after the news of the retreat was announced, instead of Mr. Conroy taking assembly, the Principal of The Tech 'Joch' Aberdeen, stepped up on to the brick parapet. Mr. Aberdeen a big man, stood tall and gave an impassioned speech to us all with the opening words that I will never forget. "Boys, England has her back to the wall, but will never be defeated!" He then went on to tell us how we should look upon the conflict that was occurring between the forces of good and evil, and do everything we could to help the war effort in any way we could. News was also coming through of the Nazi concentration camps and The Tech got the nickname of 'the concentration camp' because of it being enclosed by the high cyclone wire fence, and the strict rules that applied to when the gates would be open and closed to let students in and out.

In June Italy declared war on the Allies, a decision that had long been expected, so we thought that this was why we did not see the likable, Italian student Lorenzo again at The Tech, probably he and his family were in an internment camp together with the Germans. Another event of great significance happened in 1940; 'The Battle of Britain' commenced in July. Not only were we getting the news from the papers and the local radio, but we also listened intently on my father's short wave radio to the BBC, and a German radio station broadcasting in English. It broadcast very different war news than that which we heard on the BBC, local radio and read in newspapers. This was a stark example of hearing both sides of the story, but of course we treated the version we heard on German radio 'with a grain of salt' or more exactly as untrue, being described by the word 'propaganda. One of the German announcers was an Englishman and was nicknamed Lord Haw Haw.

Towards the end of the year we were notified that the (CVTSS) was on again and this time they were to be held at Castlemaine. Of course I was delighted and had no trouble getting permission and the money for a ticket from my parents and booking in to go. This time I looked at a map to see where Castlemaine was and found it to be further north than Ballarat, and on a different railway line than that to Ballarat. Eventually the sport's day came around and I said goodbye to my parents and took the train to

Spencer Street, ready to set out on my next big railway adventure. This time however, I missed out getting a window seat, but I could see where we were going well enough to know that again the train passed through Footscray, and I was off again over that distant horizon. Very soon at Sunshine the train left the Ballarat line and turned to the north. I heard the same exciting sounds of the engine's whistle and the clickety-clicking of the wheels going over the rail joints, so even without a window seat I was very happy. The train climbed a long incline and across a forest of gum trees where Mt Macedon rose up, a mountain that I knew quite well because it is easily seen on the western horizon from above Heidelberg. The train passed through the town of Woodend and not long after another long climb, our carriage was suddenly enveloped in darkness as the train went through the long Elphinstone tunnel, and very soon after we had arrived in Castlemaine.

As before we were taken by a teacher to the Castlemaine sports ground and together with a few friends we ate our lunch. We watched the sports for a while until we got bored, then we decided to go and explore the city of Castlemaine. There were no teachers around so off we went into the city. After looking at the shops for a while we came to a picture theatre that was showing a film called *Waterloo Bridge*. We decided in a flash to go to the show that was just about to start. It starred Robert Taylor and Vivien Leigh and I thought it was a great film. Fancy travelling to Castlemaine to go to the Tech School sports and finishing up in a picture theatre for our entertainment, but that was what we did.

After the pictures finished, although we had no idea when the train would depart to take us back home, but from our experience of last year, we decided that we had better be back at the station by 4 30 p.m. We consumed a couple of beaut ice creams and wandered around the main street of Castlemaine a much smaller city and less grand than Ballarat, with very few large, imposing buildings such as

I had seen in Ballarat. We finally made our way to the station with plenty of time to spare for the supposed 4.30 p.m. assembly time.

Together with many other boys I had time to have a good look at the A^2 simmering away with the familiar pulsating sound of the air compressor's panting, keeping the brake lines full of air for the train's brakes. I was gradually learning a lot about trains and how they worked, locomotives, signalling and everything you could imagine about trains around the world, because for my birthday I had been given a wonderful book, *The Iron Road The Wonders of Railway Progress* by Cecil J. Allen, M.Inst.T. I still have this book today, well worn, but very readable.

The supervision by our teachers on this sports day was very lax. Once again there were a couple of teachers waiting on the platform who were a little unsteady on their feet. At 5 p.m. we were given permission to board the train and there was the usual scurry to get a good seat and luckily I scored a window seat. This year I had the good sense to bring along a pair of goggles and nearly all the way back to Melbourne I had my head out the window, so this time I was impervious to the bits of stinging coal that rained down on my face. I think the only time I pulled my head in was after watching the A^2 labour slowly up the steep climb amid clouds of steam, towards the Elphinstone tunnel, where I quickly pulled my head in to avoid it being hit by the very close side of the tunnel. Suddenly, a loud voice yelled out. "Close the window!" I quickly complied with the request as smoke and steam began coming through the window. I opened the window again as soon as the train was through the tunnel.

What was going on inside the carriage however, was nearly as interesting as what I was seeing outside the window, because a teacher in our compartment (not one of our teachers I hasten to say), had climbed up on to one of the long luggage racks and was lying on it trying to sleep. He didn't have much hope of getting to sleep, because he was being tickled and harassed by the students in our compartment. I was not sure if he was one of the unsteady teachers I had seen on the platform, but this one certainly had had too much to drink. When I look back on that scene, I find it hard to believe that there was not a teacher in charge who could assert some authority to prevent this sad state of affairs. There were only a few teachers who were visibly affected, but the bad example they set for us students was inexcusable. When the train was not far from Melbourne another teacher came in to our compartment and coaxed him down from the rack and took him away along the corridor, and I never saw him again.

Soon the sun went down and it was dark, but I continued watching the signals and other interesting line side items of interest. In the darkness I knew when the fireman shovelled coal into the firebox, because the orange glow of the fire could be seen at the side opening of the cab. From the number of times I saw this occur, I knew that firing a steam locomotive was not a very easy job. There was one long section of the line that for quite a few miles, the train made a roaring noise as it sped along. I learned many years later that this loud roaring sound was produced by the wheels running over the rails along this section of track, and that the phenomenon was in fact called 'roaring rails', which was caused by a faulty batch of rails made in Germany before the war.

At last the train pulled into Spencer Street station and I caught the train home in the dark, which at that time was not unusual or dangerous for a twelve year old lad to do. The trains to Rosanna only ran at hourly and half hourly intervals depending on the time of day. Sometimes I walked home from Heidelberg, but not in the dark, because the route was hilly with only the very first and last parts past have any semblance of light, but not from street lights, from a few houses. The remainder of the mile long walk was trackless through some scrub, but near the end, a creek with steep sides, with very little water in it, had to be crossed.

So I waited for a train to Rosanna and when I arrived home, my parents took one astonished look at me and asked. "Where have you been, what have you been doing?" "Why?" I asked. They said that my face was black all except my eyes. I told them how I had had my head out the train window most of the time from Castlemaine, and how I had a pair of goggles with me to keep the coal dust out of my eyes. After telling my parents all about the sports day I went and washed myself, my face especially. No more than that, because we had a shower but no hot water system. Then it was off to bed after an exciting, but unusual day at my second Tech school sports.

My second year at The Tech came to an end and I passed all the subjects with a high enough grade to get my Junior Technical Certificate, which pleased me and my family, no end. The war was continuing with its ups and downs, the Battle of Britain resulting in the destruction of many cities in England and Germany with the loss of many lives. I am sure I did not understand the enormity and tragedy of the war at the time, which was probably a good thing for my peace of mind and the exciting life I was leading away from The Tech with the Scouts.

In January 1941 my parents rented part of a house on Point Nepean Road Edithvale. Donald and I took our luggage down to the Rosanna station in a billy cart in the morning and this was sent by train to Edithvale. We left with more luggage just after lunch and when we got to Edithvale the luggage was there waiting for us. It was the height of the holiday season and there were young lads at the station with billy carts, which for a small sum they took our luggage to the place we had rented. This may seem unusual today, but many families rented houses at that time of the year in towns all the way from Mordialloc to Portsea. The safe, sandy beaches along that stretch of Port Phillip Bay were ideal for young holidaying families.

The house was ideally placed for watching trains because it was directly opposite a level crossing protected by warning bells and flashing red lights. When we weren't on the beach getting sunburnt, building sand castles, or swimming, we would rush out of the house every time we heard the bells ringing. Most of the time it was only an electric train going past, but sometimes we were rewarded by seeing a much more exciting train. A troop train, usually hauled by a chugging D^3 class, with soldiers in khaki all hanging out of the windows madly waving and yelling. The troop trains we saw were either going to or coming from the Army camp at Balcombe on the Mornington Peninsula. It was a reminder that our country and our soldiers were fighting in a desperate war of survival for our way of life.

At last it was time to return to The Tech for my final year to gain my Senior Technical Certificate. The final year subjects were very interesting and varied. Some were practical subjects, Wood Working, Sheet Metal Working and also in the practical category, I should also include Chemistry. Theory subjects included Geography, Geometry, English and Mathematics. I had a very good idea what I wanted to be when I finished my schooling, the same as many young boys, and that was to be an engine (locomotive) driver, but as I got older I had learned from books and other sources about the very many years of menial training it took, beginning with being an engine cleaner. I felt that although I certainly would have liked to have become an engine driver, it seemed as though it was not the sort of work experience that I would enjoy, to attain the thrilling, ultimate goal of driving one of the most marvellous machines that has ever been invented. I did however think that I would like to work in the railways, but at what I was not quite sure.

As the year progressed I enjoyed my studies and sport, still playing baseball in the field at the back of the school. One day a ball went over the top of my glove and hit my mouth. I didn't think any damage had been done, but over the years my front top tooth died and gradually went black. It finally fell out many years later and I had to get a top plate to replace it. Further along St. Georges Road there was a swimming pool and sometimes we went there for sport. This pool, unlike Heidelberg State School's pool was chlorinated, but I think I preferred the untreated water of my old school, because the chlorine affected my eyes.

The Tech soon became full to overflowing and a couple of temporary class rooms were placed inside, and to one side of the quadrangle. On some days due to the overcrowding, our class of about twenty boys walked about a mile to the West Preston primary school where we had classes there. English was one of the subjects I studied in one of the temporary classrooms at the side of the quadrangle. Our teacher was a young bloke who had a beautiful, big brown, English setter dog with him and the dog would sit contentedly and obediently at his master's side on the platform during the class.

We were studying the period novel *Ivanhoe* by Sir Walter Scott. The story did not make much of an impression on me as the plot was quite complicated. The exploits of the hero Ivanhoe from which the book got its name, was of interest because Ivanhoe was where my Ivanhoe Gram lived, but I do not know if the novel *Ivanhoe* was where the name Ivanhoe came from. The war was being fought along many fronts, in particular Africa where many of our Australian soldiers were fighting against the Germans in the desert. Our English teacher told us a little about this war and where it was taking place, and I found this much more interesting with direct consequences to our country and soldiers than Ivanhoe in his battles with the Normans.

The practical classes were more to my liking and understanding. The Woodworking class rooms at the far end of the school were well equipped and I enjoyed working with wood, but having to watch out for the way the grain ran so that the wood did not split where it wasn't supposed to, was a bit of a bugbear.

However, my favourite practical class was undoubtedly Sheet Metal, where I made something that worked, a small boiler, which was brought to the boil by a little kerosene burner underneath. The steam that was produced was directed through a small tube and drove a small bladed turbine that I made. A cork was used as a safety valve in the boilers the class made, preventing any of them from blowing up and injuring us. I was however, injured in the class, not by a boiler blowing up, but by one stupid classmate who put a warm piece of metal on the back of my neck. It didn't really hurt much and I quickly removed it and turned around and swore vehemently at him. On the way home on my bike I felt the back of my neck and a big blister had formed, which my mother bathed and put some ointment on it, but It took a while to go down.

Nevertheless it was in this class that I realised how much I enjoyed working with my hands and with metal that had no grain. That sheet metal class was really responsible for directing me along the path that my life took after I left The Tech. I loved forming the metal with various tools and soldering them all together. Chemistry was another practical subject I studied. I found that the experiments we did were very interesting. We had a foreign teacher-certainly not a German as they had all been interned. He was a nice bloke with a bit of a sense of humour. We did many experiments using U tubes. One experiment involved having the U tube filled with water and observing the difference in the height of the water in each leg when the legs were subjected to various conditions. When we drew the U tube he told us to: "Put 'H' for the height of the water column, not HELL ha ha ha," which I think his former class students must have been doing.

Another experiment I remember doing in his class was catching a fly, not an easy task, then putting it into a glass beaker and closing the top. After a while when the fly's movements had slowed down, some oxygen from an oxygen bottle was piped into the beaker and to our amazement, gradually, the fly began to move around even more rapidly than before it was put in the beaker. I wondered afterwards if we had caught a fly with fly spray and put it in the beaker when it was not quite dead, would oxygen have brought it back to life...This experiment came to mind many times in later years, because as well as books on trains and meteorology that I read, I was very interested in books on mountaineering, especially Mt Everest and the mountains of the Himalayas where oxygen was used to help climbers combat the shortage of oxygen at high altitudes. Although we did many interesting experiments and tests, I had learned enough in the class to know that Chemistry was not going to be my vocation in life. Our teacher was a great bloke and a good teacher whatever his nationality. Looking back I tend to think he was Hungarian.

Spring came around again. The time when an announcement was usually made about the (CVTSS), but this year the sports were not going to be held in a big city over the horizon, but at a sports ground in Dandenong, if my memory serves me correctly. I was not interested in going because it did not involve an exciting, long, train journey so that was the end of those wonderful train rides and exploring two of Victoria's largest regional cities. I imagined that the railways were too busy carrying troops to various places like I had seen at Edithvale, and were very busy performing many other essential railway tasks required for the war, which was now in its third year.

The end of my schooling at The Tech came all too quickly as I had enjoyed every day of my schooling there. My days too, of riding my bike along Bell Street were over. For all of those three years of riding I had not had any accidents, nor had my bike suffered any breakdowns except of course for the occasional puncture. I left The Tech a very happy fourteen year old proudly bearing my Senior Technical Certificate.

CHAPTER 5

A NEW TECH AND MODEL RAILWAYS 1942

Not long after I left The Tech on December 7th 1941, the Japanese bombed the American naval base at Pearl Harbour and America entered the war. We all felt that now that America had declared war on the Germans and Japanese and America had become one of the Allies, the course of the war would we hoped, turn in our favour, so the year 1941 ended with a more optimistic outlook.

I busied myself during the holidays going on bike rides sometimes with the Scouts and other times by myself. A usual we went to Edithvale for our annual holidays, but this time after I had helped take our luggage to the station on the billy cart, I rode my bike to Edithvale, while the rest of the family followed in the train. It was a great idea to ride my bike there because I was able to go on many bike rides around Edithvale and along Point Nepean Road. I was still very interested in the trains that went past and this year not only did I see troop trains and a train full of sailors, but I even saw a train with tanks loaded on flat cars, indicating that the pace of the war involving our country had increased considerably.

In the New Year the question for me and my parents was what I should do next to further my education. Because there was no doubt that my interest lay in engineering. My parents suggested that I should go to the Royal Melbourne Technical College and see what courses were available for me there. Dressed in my Preston Tech short trouser uniform, my mother took me in to the Royal Melbourne Technical College (RMTC) as it was called then in 1942. We had an interview with one of the college course advisers, and although he thought I was a little young to begin a five year Engineering Diploma course. Because of my interest in engineering, he said I should enrol in a three year Mechanical Engineering Certificate course. If I did well he said that I could then study for a Diploma. That seemed to be the way to go so I was enrolled to begin classes in February. The subjects I would be learning to begin with were Chemistry, Engineering Drawing, Mathematics I (Algebra), Trigonometry and Geometry

I suppose it was not surprising given my interest and love of railways that sooner or later I would be looking at getting a model railway of some sort. I have a photo of my first train set taken when I was about three years old. It was a small Hornby tinplate track with a wind up locomotive and a couple of carriages all made of tin. The photo shows me playing with it on the front lawn with my Ivanhoe Gram looking on.

The author with his first train set

My father was interested in trains and when I told him that I would like to get a model train set he said. "OK we will see what we can do." One day in January before my father went back to work he took me to visit all of the model shops that were in the city. Herbert Small's shop on the corner of Elizabeth and Collins Streets sold models of all sorts, model cars, Hornby trains, Meccano sets and the like. Another model shop called the Model Dockyard was located downstairs in a basement in Swanston Street near the corner of Bourke Street. It was run by a short, grey haired, old man who wore a ship captain's hat. The side of the stairs leading down to the shop in the basement was lined with glass cases containing many fabulous models of sailing ships. On reaching the bottom of the stairs and entering the shop, a wonderland of models was revealed. There was a spectacular assortment of model trains of various sizes held in a row of glass cases at hip level, while around the shop there were many sailing ships in full sail displayed in all their glory. I did not want to leave the shop as I was in complete awe of what I was seeing, but my father said there was still another model shop to visit, the Meadmore Model Engineering Company in Exhibition Street just around the corner from Swanston Street above Cox Brothers.

This shop was of a different style to Smalls and the Model Dockyard. It sold American model trains, more expensive and larger detailed models than were to be seen in the other two shops. It was from this shop however, that my father got some good hints on how to build a model railway. My father said that soon he would begin to construct a model train layout in my bedroom. I really think that it was not only me that wanted a train set, but that my father was as keen as I was to have one. I was thrilled and said I would help him.

On February 19th 1942 Darwin was bombed by the Japanese, which was a great shock to our people and government. In February too, my classes began at the RMTC. I went by train to Princes Bridge and left the station up the stairs to Russel Street and from there walked up Russel Street to the RMTC. Many times in the coming days I would stop for a minute or two to watch the fireman shovel coal into the boilers of the Royal Melbourne Hospital on the corner of Latrobe Street. I was dressed not in my Preston Tech uniform with short trousers, but long, grey trousers and a shirt and tie. Very soon however, I discarded the tie as none of the other students wore one. Such a thing as Jeans, those God forsaken, 'blue', ragged, item of ubiquitous clothing had not been invented and on the whole students, even without a tie, were casually, but well dressed. I began classes and the first subject that springs to mind was Engineering Drawing. During the course of my education many of my teacher's names and their appearance readily spring to mind, but others I have lost in the storeroom of my memory. One teacher that I have never forgotten was Francis William Tough, a short, middle aged, gentleman with a big moustache who took my class of Engineering Drawing. He had written a very good instruction book that we used in class. As well as the theory topics that applied to the practise of Engineering Drawing, I really enjoyed sitting at a drawing board with a T square and drawing various shapes with a sharp pencil, rule, compass, triangle and square. Then applying dimensions to the shapes according to the simple methods illustrated in Francis William's excellent book. As I remember the war did not make much of an impact on my schooling.

Chemistry on the other hand I did not find as interesting. This subject was taught in the huge wooden, amphitheatre like, grandstand in Building 1, which also contained the offices fronting Latrobe Street and Bowen Square. Our teacher was Mr. Watson an irascible, grey haired, bloke. This class was the first class that I had ever been in that had female students.

I will never forget the opening address that Mr. Watson gave to the class, in which he singled out the young ladies in the class in a very sexist manner. He said that if the females in the class expected to study this subject, he would be discussing the London Sewerage System. He said; "You will have to get used to the use of terms such as excreta, faeces and the like." I somehow got the feeling that Mr. Watson had never taught a dual sex class before. However the classes went along during the year, with as he had said, one of the topics was the London Sewerage System, which I found very interesting. I am sure the young ladies in the class did also, but there wasn't too much emphasis in his lecture on the words that Mr. Watson had used in his opening address.

The rest of the Chemistry topics were about the various elements, their symbols and how they combined to form compounds, some of which were a little beyond my understanding, especially strings of chemical equations. Algebra and Trigonometry were subjects I enjoyed, especially working out problems using the trigonometric tables. Geometry too, like Trigonometry were in a sense practical subjects dealing with various solid shapes, pyramids, cones and spheres, and the formulas that applied to each geometrical form. Our Geometry teacher was a tall, well-built bloke by the name of Mr. Proudfoot. Once when he was standing in front of the class telling us about some feature of Geometry, he suddenly lurched to one side of his body and grabbed his left knee! Looking up towards our startled class he said with a pained expression on his face: "Sorry lads, it's my old football injury, it happens every now and again." He sat down and after a short time stood up and went on with the lesson from the point where he was suddenly interrupted. And yes, it did happen again a couple of times during the year I spent in his class.

From an *Encyclopaedia of Australian Rules Football Players*, I found that there were only three players by the name of Proudfoot who had played the game. Only one I thought could have been our Geometry teacher. Alec Proudfoot who played two games with St. Kilda in 1926-27, and one game with Melbourne in 1929. His football career I imagine was cut short because he badly injured his knee and in those days, it was the end of playing football. I like to think that Alec Proudfoot was in fact, my Geometry teacher.

My first year at the RMTC progressed, doing well in subjects I enjoyed, and not so well in those I didn't. Back home my father was progressing with the construction of our model railway layout. He had bought some 4 inch wide, tongue and groove, wood battens and planned to construct a large circular layout to fit in my bedroom. He cut the wood in sections and joined them together with mortised joints held together firmly with black rivets inserted in holes drilled in the mortised joints. There were various gauges of models on sale at the time, the most popular gauge being 'O' gauge 1¼ inches (31.25 mm) between the rails. There were two other smaller gauges available 'HO' and 'OO', but 'O' gauge he felt was the best for us. As well as laying the two running rails, a method of supplying power (low voltage DC) to model locomotives so that they could be operated by a line side controller, was provided by means of a third rail laid in the centre, or the outside of the running rails. My father chose the centre rail option. When the layout was complete and we purchased our first locomotive, it would collect the power for its motor from the centre rail by means of a roller fitted to the bottom of the locomotive.

Next he purchased from one of the model shops, all the items required to lay the track. Brass bullhead rails, pre-cut sleepers, chairs to attach the rail to the sleepers, and fishplates to connect the rails. As well he purchased a tool to insert the very small tacks to secure the chairs to the sleepers and a track gauge to make sure the rails were laid exactly 1¼ inches apart. As can be imagined my father was a wonderful man. His Christian name was also Gordon the same name as mine. I have kept my memory of him with me. as I now sign my name Gordon Smith II. It was a great thrill to help him whenever I could and I learned a lot about using various tools as he put together the layout.

Donald my younger brother who was ten years old at the time also helped, although he was not as interested in trains as I was. I was studying hard to get a pass at the end of the year in Chemistry, but I had no admiration for our teacher Mr. Watson, and I think this did not help my appreciation of the subject, although I enjoyed Chemistry at the Preston Tech and liked our foreign teacher who taught me there. Travelling to the RMTC each day on the train was very relaxing and I got plenty of time to read books on trains and mountains and do a bit of Chemistry study. There were very few steam trains running on our Heidelberg line and I was only able to see some steam locomotives when the train entered the tracks leading to Princess Bridge station. K, D^3 and A^2 were the most common classes I saw.

I had also learned to recognise the various types of wheel arrangements of each locomotive and that knowledge made my observations much more interesting. Locomotives types can be described in many ways, tender, tank, passenger, goods or shunting locomotives, but common to all these descriptive terms is the arrangement of their wheels, which is called the 'wheel arrangement' of a locomotive. All steam locomotives have large driving wheels connected together and powered by steam pressure in the cylinders. Some locomotives only have driving wheels, but most also have four or two in front to guide and support the front of the locomotive. Some also have two or four small wheels behind the driving wheels that help support the rear of the locomotive boiler and firebox. Three wheel arrangement examples are as follows:

4-6-2   This arrangement of numbers separated by dashes, is the wheel arrangement of the S class *Spirit of Progress* locomotives, four wheels in front of the driving wheels, six driving wheels and two wheels at the rear of the driving wheels. Many wheel arrangements are given names, and in this case the name given to this wheel arrangement is 'Pacific.'

0-6-0   This is the wheel arrangement of Y and E class tank locomotives, which only have driving wheels.

2-8-0   This is the wheel arrangement of C and K class locomotives and the name given to this wheel arrangement is 'Consolidation.'

The second half of my first year at the RMTC was much like the first half. I still struggled with Chemistry, but all the other subjects were well within my control. The final exams came along and I passed all of the subjects except Chemistry, which was a pity, but really no surprise. My parents were hopeful that I would do better in the next year of the course. I enrolled to repeat Chemistry and study some new subjects, Applied Mechanics, Fluid mechanics, Heat Engines and Mathematics II. I decided I would really study in 1942 and surprise myself and my parents by passing every subject, even Chemistry. That was my intention anyway.

At the beginning of 1942 I continued with my certificate course at the RMTC. After Darwin was bombed in February 1942 and then on 31st May 1942, miniature Japanese submarines entered Sydney Harbour causing extensive damage, we realised that the war was now getting much nearer to us in Victoria. The 'brownout' was declared in Victoria and in all the other states., It involved all street lighting being reduced in brightness and neon signs being shut off. Many houses had blacked out their windows, but we didn't bother. Motorists were fitting headlight shields over their headlights, which only allowed a small rectangular section of the headlight beam to show and above the opening, a small extension prevented light from being seen from above. Motorists were restricted in their use of cars because of petrol rationing so the number of cars seen on the roads as a consequence was greatly reduced. A 'brownout,' was not as severe as a full 'blackout', which was being experienced in England.

At night when I rode my bike to Scouts it was enthralling and rather scary watching search lights weaving a pattern over Melbourne. A device called a dynamo was used to generate electricity to light the head and tail lights of my bike. The dynamo was rigidly attached to a back fork of the bike with its small, serrated, driving wheel mounted just clear of the rim of the tyre. By releasing a catch, this allowed the small drive wheel to come in spring loaded contact with the rim of the tyre, producing about 4 volts to light the lamps, but only when the bike was moving. When the dynamo was in operation, it made it noticeably harder to push the bike, but today's bike lighting systems are much, much, safer and efficient and require no extra energy output from the cyclist.

My father stopped making the railway set and turned his attention to building an air raid shelter in the large back yard of our house. Of course we all helped him and eventually the air raid shelter we dug was about 3 feet wide, 10 feet long and 4 feet deep, no easy job in heavy clay soil. Sheets of galvanised iron were placed over the top of the shelter and a pile of dirt on top of the iron. The shelter was filled with various items of food and clothing, but no weapons. Householders were urged by the government to do this and many that we knew complied

The author's father in uniform

with this advice. My father was 42 years of age and missed the call up because he was married and had three children to look after, however he joined some form of reserve army. I can remember him in his army uniform complete with slouch hat.

Our next door neighbours on one side were a lovely middle aged, English couple, Mr. and Mrs. Downs. Their son Jack had enlisted and was in England. They received letters from him saying he was in Bomber Command as a navigator, and it was about this time that the Downs got the sad news that Jack was missing in action. We felt for his parents and tried to cheer them up as best we could, saying that he was a probably a prisoner of war and they would soon hear that he was safe.

Sometimes I went on scout camps to Janefield and Dromana with the Scouts and also to the Gilwell Scout Park. We travelled to Gilwell in a furniture van that was fitted with detachable bench seats, a very common and cheap mode of transport in those days that was used to take people to Sunday school picnics and other recreational outings.

The furniture van taking us to Gilwell operated on what was called producer gas, carbon monoxide, produced by the burning of charcoal in a gas producer. This was a boiler type unit either attached to a vehicle or in the case of our furniture van, fitted on a trailer towed along behind. I remember vividly, the driver clad in dirty overalls, stopping a couple of times on the way, getting out and refuelling the gas producer from a bag of charcoal carried on the trailer. This was certainly much harder and dirtier than filling from a petrol bowser, although the engine had to be started on petrol and then, when it was going it was switched over to gas. During the war many of these units were fitted to commercial vehicles and private cars too. I had seen photos taken during the war in England of this gas stored in huge bags carried on the roof of cars and piped to the engine, but had not seen one of these here.

Walking through the streets of Melbourne on the way to and from the MTC, many soldiers and sailors in uniform were to be seen, even sometimes Americans in uniform. It was reported that the railways were under great stress trying to keep up with the transport of people, troops and goods. All railway rolling stock, locomotives, passenger carriages and goods wagons were at a premium and many were being taken out of retirement and being pressed into service in support of the war effort. The Australian railway system's Achilles's heel, the break of gauges between the various states, was proving a problem in the essential, efficient distribution of domestic and war supplies, particularly at the border town of Albury between Victoria and New South Wales.

I continued with my studies at the RMTC and was now the proud possessor of a slide rule, which together with various tables were the necessary tools of the time for calculation needs in class. I was having difficulty understanding all the topics of the two main

Engineering subjects, Applied Mechanics that was all about structures and calculating the forces and their direction in various forms of trusses, cantilevers, box girders and the like. The study of the design and calculation of riveted joints, used in the fabrication of the structures, although very interesting, I found hard to master. Fluid Mechanics was based on Archimedes Principal, which I fully understood. The topics were mainly about vessels that float in water and their design, where in the vessels, their centre of gravity and their centre of buoyancy lay. I found the subject fascinating and understood most all that I was being taught.

The other subjects Mathematics II was Calculus. Our teacher was a foreigner, I think Polish, who wore thick black glasses to go with his huge head of unruly black hair. He had a delightful accent, but was easy to understand, both his words and the subject of Calculus. Heat Engines was a great practical subject, where our class went down into a large laboratory room filled with engines, mostly diesel and petrol. We learned about the two and four stroke cycles and how each engine operated. Most interesting was operating some of the engines and taking indicator diagrams of their horsepower outputs. As far as I remember there was not a steam engine in the laboratory, which was a bit of a pity. Our instructor was a likable man, small in stature called Sid Sears, who had a bit of a lisp, but that did not detract from his teaching ability.

Repeating Chemistry was no fun at all because I did not like the subject, or Mr. Watson. I made sure I attended the first lecture to see if he singled out the female students with his London Sewerage System remarks, but thankfully he didn't, although there were some young ladies in the class. I attended many of the lectures, but my understanding of the subject was still not great. To my knowledge, I don't know if Mr. Watson discussed the London Sewerage System, but with the Blitz taking place in London at the time, I would have thought that the sewerage system would have been severely damaged. It may have been one of the lectures I missed, because I got a little bored and began going to the museum, the library and to 'the pictures,' the slang word used to describe the movies. I usually went to *The Capital theatre* in Swanston Street where I saw many great films. Some I remember were *The Road to Zanzibar, The Man Who Came to Dinner,* and *Union Pacific* a great American railroad story.

I had in the back of my mind that one day I should go along to Spencer Street station and see *The Spirit* arrive in Spencer Street at 11.30 a.m. from Albury, or leave for Albury at 6.30 p.m. in the evening, which I was sure would be a grand experience to see. I finally put my thoughts into action and decided that seeing *The Spirit* arrive would be more convenient. I chose a morning when I only had an afternoon class and I took the train to Spencer Street arriving there about 30 minutes before The Spirit was due to arrive at 11.30. It was announced on the PA that *The Spirit* was on time, so I walked along to the far west end of number one platform to get the first view of the train as it came through North Melbourne.

Right on time the beautiful, blue front of the locomotive with smoke and steam coming from its chimney appeared in the distance. Very soon I could see the royal blue, carriages of the train as it threaded its way across the suburban tracks, finally straightening up as it headed for number one platform. It slowly approached where I was standing on the platform and I could feel the heat from the S class as it went past me with the beautiful royal blue and gold striped train in its wake, eventually coming to a smooth stop down the far end of the platform. I quickly strode along the platform past the carriages towards the S class and stood in awe in front of the locomotive admiring the streamlining, which I must say, was rather grimy. I walked along by the side of S class and despite the grime the streamlined side of the locomotive was a picture of iconic grandeur, with the brass letters of its name shining proudly on its side, but sadly I cannot remember which of the four explorer's names it was. I then moved along and stood looking up at the driver and fireman in the cab hoping that I might be invited into the cab, but they completely ignored me. They had good reason to, because I noticed that a shunter had just climbed back on the platform after disconnecting the baggage car from the rest of the train. He gave a signal to the driver and with a short blast on the whistle, with clouds of steam coming from the front of the S class it slowly moved forward towards the buffers with the baggage car.

I decided that I wanted to have a look at *The Spirit* carriages so I walked slowly along the platform peering through the windows into the beautifully upholstered seats, polished wooden panels and fittings in the compartments. About half way along the train I came to a shunter who was standing by an open door and I asked him if I could have a look inside. He said. "I'm about to take the train around the loop, would you like to come with me?" I blurted out a quick "Yes thanks and he invited me to climb aboard. I couldn't believe my luck. A minute or so later the shunter waved his green flag and with an answering whistle from a locomotive up front that had coupled itself to the parlour or observation car, that I choose to call it, we very slowly began to move along the platform in the direction of North Melbourne.

The shunter explained to me that the locomotive, a D4 class shunting locomotive was taking *The Spirit* around the reversing loop at the rear of the North Melbourne locomotive sheds and that when we arrived back in number one platform *The Spirit* carriages would be facing the right way to begin its journey to Albury at 6.30 p.m.. As *The Spirit* was slowly hauled around the loop I went and sat in one of the beautifully appointed compartments, but I wasn't sure whether it was first or second class. I looked out of the large window and it was interesting to see various locomotives stored behind the sheds and spare wheels and other parts of rolling stock stored there.

We had to wait a short time after leaving the loop for the signalman to find us a path across the tracks and back to number one platform, where *The Spirit* was brought to a stop the right way round. Before it was due to leave for Albury at 6.30. p.m. it would be thoroughly cleaned, together with many other servicing and maintenance tasks required to bring it back to pristine condition after its long journey from Albury. I thanked the shunter profusely and we parted with a firm handshake. I left *The Spirit* there and realised I was a little late for my class, but that was not important, I had just had the privilege of taking at unique journey around a railway line that was an integral part of the story of the *Spirit of Progress*. More than that I realised that I had had a ride on the fabulous *Spirit of Progress*! There was no loop in Albury to turn *The Spirit;* instead there was a large triangle of railway lines, together with sets of points that served the same purpose of reversing the train.

I sat for the exams at the end of the year with some surprising and some not so surprising results. I failed in both Fluid Mechanics and Applied Mechanics, but passed in Chemistry, due to my study, with no thanks to Mr. Watson. I also passed Heat Engines, and couldn't believe I had passed Calculus with quite a high mark. Some achievement I thought, although my parents were a little disappointed at the overall result, and of course so was I. The two subjects, Fluid Mechanics and Applied Mechanics were key academic subjects in which to gain passes, if I was to qualify for a Mechanical Engineering Certificate, let alone a Diploma.

My parents and I gave my further education some thought and it was decided that I should take a year off and see what the New Year held in the way of getting a job, or furthering my education in some other field. It was a month or so before Christmas and my father went back to building our train set and shortly before Christmas it was complete. It took up most of my bedroom. The layout was in the shape of a U with the top end closed, with the same curve as the bottom of the U. The straight, far side of the track ran under my bed and a rectangular piece had to be cut out of the bottom of the door to allow the door to open and close. My father went to the Meadmore Model Engineering Company's shop and bought home all the catalogues of the model locomotives they sold. I can remember to this day pouring over the beautiful coloured catalogues showing models of *The Lincoln Zephyr*, the stunning, silver, diesel train and the equally stunning streamlined, art deco styled, *Hiawatha* locomotive and train. These two model trains depicted in the catalogue brought to life, two famous American trains that I had read about and seen photos of in my train books. We decided that one of the Lionel model steam locomotives and tender illustrated in the catalogue would be the one to begin running on our layout.

One day my father came home with a thrilling surprise for us, me in particular. He had bought the locomotive we had decided on and the control box to operate it. He said that it was an advance Christmas present. We all crowded round in my room, and after we had unpacked the locomotive and tender

A Lional Locomotive similar to the authors

we put it carefully on the rails and connected the power. By means of a button and a sliding control we soon discovered how to start, stop, reverse and control the speed of the locomotive. It was a great thrill after all the hours and work my father had put in to see the locomotive and tender run around the layout. It must also have been a great sense of achievement for my father to see the locomotive going round his track without any hint of a problem, after all the many hours he had spent building the layout. We spent the next hour or two having fun watching the locomotive go round and round the layout. The model was based on an American type of locomotive 2-4-2 wheel arrangement and looked very powerful. I decided that I would have to see about purchasing some rolling stock to go with the locomotive.

The war events that occurred during 1942 saw many gains and losses. The fall of Singapore to the Japanese was a great set back bringing the war a little closer to Australia, but the Americans had won a decisive sea battle at Midway and the war in the African desert saw great advances for the Allies on this front.

The 1943 New Year celebrations were rather subdued although the war was finally looking a little more promising for the Allies. We went on our yearly holiday to Edithvale, eating apricots for nearly every meal; getting sunburnt and watching the trains go by, noting that there were more troop trains than last year. In February, back home after the holidays, my father employed a carpenter to install windows in the front veranda and this was to become my bedroom, while Donald and Geoff, my two brothers, spaced five years apart were to have beds in a big room that led to the front verandah. This left my former bedroom with open access to the train layout, together with a number of desks and cupboards arranged along the opposite wall.

Early in the New Year I graduated from the Scouts to the Rover Scouts. Being a member of the Rover Scouts was to lead me to paths that had a great influence on my life in many respects. Now that I had my own sleep-out I decided to start building my first model to run on our layout. I chose to build a model VR guard's van, a 'Z' van as they are appropriately classified. Whatever other rolling stock we eventually got for the layout, the last wagon always has to be a Z van (in goods trains anyhow). In my front veranda sleep out I had a clothes cupboard, a big wireless set and at the far end a table and it was on this that I began making my Z van. I acquired a set of crude plans for the Z van from a railway magazine, and I took some photographs of the vans whenever the opportunity arose, usually in a siding at the Heidelberg railway station. With my pocket money I bought a small soldering iron, flux, solder, some small files and other odd tools. I used wood cut from a butter box for the body and some left over bull head rails for the frame and the shunter's running boards on the side of the van. My model Z van was coming along splendidly, and I devoted all my spare time during the day and night to completing it and have the joy of seeing it run on our layout behind the locomotive.

The war was still experiencing periods of highs and lows for the Allies. In February the Germans surrendered at Stalingrad, but in March there were 27 merchant ships sunk by German U boats, which was a great loss, as supplies from America were vital for the war effort and life in the UK. Although of course it had to be kept a secret at the time, a most important event occurred when code breakers at Bletchley Park in England, managed to break the German codes, a massive achievement that allowed the Allies to track Donitz's submarine fleet and many other movements of the various German forces.

Rosanna was a small township with four shops, a news agent-grocer, a greengrocer-confectioner and a butcher shop on Lower Plenty Road across from the railway station. Facing the station there was Freddie Kingston's boot maker's shop. My father and a few others, if they were early for the train, would go into the shop while they waited for the train to arrive and discuss all manner of subjects with Freddie, mainly sport I would think. Just below the shops, Lower Plenty Road crossed the railway line and the warning of an approaching train was by means of a 'wig–wag,' a swinging red disc, with a red light at its centre, together with the ringing of a loud bell. It was a very good warning device in those years, before the advent of automatic boom gates. We lived nearly at the top of our aptly named road Hillside Road. It was discovered that from our elevated front porch, if we directed our gaze to the rising ground between the Macleod and Watsonia Railway Stations, we could see a train emerge through a stand of trees and begin its descent to the Macleod Railway Station. If we left home as soon as the train was seen and briskly walked down Hillside Road to the railway station, we would arrive there just before the train. Many times my mother would stand there, and mainly for my father's benefit if he was running late in the mornings. As soon as my mother saw the train come out of the trees she would yell out. "The train, the train!" Then my father would quickly go down to the station just in time to catch the train.

On Saturday mornings I managed to get work helping the local fruitier Mr. Wines deliver vegetables from his truck. This earned me the princely sum of two shillings for the morning's work. I enjoyed the work meeting housewives in their kitchens. Some of the money helped me to buy parts for the Z van, parts that I could not make myself, wheels, buffers, couplings and the like. My father was great friends with Mr. Goller who lived not far away in the next street, and he was the President of the Preston Baseball Club. My father asked him if I could get a game of baseball with his club and soon I was invited to join a game at a paddock in East Preston.

The author in his baseball uniform

After I had finished delivering the fruit, I rode my bike over to the diamond in a paddock in East Preston and played baseball with the Preston Baseball Club, (the thirds I believe). I played a number of games there and with the club at various other baseball fields, Spotswood being one of them. I was never really any good at the game; I was too small and did not have a strong throwing arm. The only reason I got a game was because most of the regular team were in the armed forces. The highlight of my baseball career was when I played at the St Kilda football ground near St. Kilda Junction, in a curtain raiser for-believe it or not; the game between Essendon and St Kilda, with my family watching me from the grandstand. That was the only Essendon football game I saw that year, because I was playing baseball instead. I still retain my love of baseball and believe that along with Australian Rules football, they are the two best team games in the world.

Apart from my job of delivering fruit, I had another couple of jobs that helped me earn my pocket money. One was mowing our lawns back and front with a push mower, not an easy task as the large front lawn was buffalo grass and the even bigger back lawn was a mixture, with a lot of union grass in it that was a Devil's own job to mow. Our back yard was long enough to accommodate a full length cricket pitch (22 yards) not an actual cricket pitch as such, just the length. I played many games of cricket there with my father and brothers, most times with a hard, regular cricket ball.

Another job, or more correctly described as an errand, was that on a Saturday night, mostly in the winter, I would run down to the station about 8 p.m. and wait for the paper train to come in. All the papers for the newsagents on our line were carried in the guard's van of a normal scheduled train, with the overflow in adjoining compartments. I would sometimes help to carry the papers up to the newsagent where there was a great throng of men and a few boys like myself, waiting excitedly for the papers to be unwrapped and purchase their papers. *The Herald, The Truth, Smith's Weekly* and the one my father wanted besides *The Herald,* The pink *Sporting Globe* 'the sport' as it was called. The *Sporting Globe* carried all the sporting news of that day and week, overseas cricket scores, horse and greyhound races, but especially the Victorian Football League (VFL) scores and stories.

Our family were great milk drinkers especially me. I did not drink tea or coffee until I went on long hikes with the Rover Scouts, and then only because there was no other option except water. After I got my bike I had another important job or errand, to ride my bike with a big milk billy can over the handlebars, up and across to the dairy about a mile away located in the cow paddocks of West Heidelberg, where the billycan was partly filled with lovely, white creamy milk. I then rode carefully home, without spilling a drop of milk. Where we got the milk from before I went on that ride a couple of times a week I was not sure, maybe it was delivered. After making some enquires later in the year about becoming a cadet with the Bureau of Meteorology, I very quickly abandoned the idea, when I discovered that I would be stationed on remote islands and other remote locations during the learning period. This left me with what at the time was really my first choice and love, a job in the railways.

CHAPTER 6

A Z VAN AND APPLYING FOR A JOB IN THE VR 1943

VICTORIAN RAILWAY APPRENTICES WANTED

The Victorian Railway Commissioners invite applications for apprentices to fill 97 vacancies in the trades of armature winder, boiler-maker, car and wagon builder, car painter, carpenter and joiner, coper smith, electrical fitter, fitter and turner, interlocking fitter, pattern maker, tin smith and sheet metal worker, and upholsterer.

The applicant must be 15 and over, but less than 18 years of age at the 10th January 1944, except those who hold the University Leaving Certificate or Technical School Diploma will be eligible to apply, provided they have not attained their nineteenth birthday on that date.

Forms of application for the positIons may be procured from the Secretary for Railways (Room 225) Spencer Street Melbourne, until 4 p.m. on 8th October

---

My father told me that he had seen an advertisement in the newspaper, (copy left) where the Victorian Railways were wanting young lads of my age to apply to become apprentices in various trades. We studied the advertisement together and it was decided that I should send away for an application form, which I did right away.

The war news at the time was very encouraging for the Allies. Italy surrendered and in the Pacific, US forces overcame the Japanese at Guadalcanal. I finished playing baseball at the end of the winter, and I was also no longer required by Mr. Wines to help with his fruit deliveries. With the better weather of spring now at hand, I spent many weekends hiking with the Rover Scouts around the nearby hills and riding my bike here and there. It did not take very long for me to receive the application form in the post from the VR, but the next day, before I had time to study the application brochure and make up my mind what trade I should apply for, I received another letter from the VR. This letter was a demand for the payment of a fine to the VR, for trespassing on railway property at Hurstbridge. I was stunned! My thoughts of becoming a railway apprentice looked like coming to an abrupt end, because at the bottom of the letter there was a note, the exact words of which I do not remember, but to the effect that any person found guilty of an offence of VR by-laws was not eligible for employment in the Victorian Railways.

My father was very angry. He took me aside and asked me to explain to him exactly how this trespass came about. I told him that after a hike that I had been on with the Rover Scouts that finished at Hurstbridge, we had to wait about one hour for the train. I went in to the railway goods yard to look at some goods wagons parked there, to help me with some details of a model I was thinking of making, after I had finished the Z van. I did not think I was doing anything wrong, but a railway officer came into the yard and took down my name and address and ordered me out of the yard.

After that, I thought nothing more of it. I went on to tell my father that when my name and address was taken, I couldn't help but notice that two railway men in VR uniforms were playing 'kick to kick' football with some young blokes who were also in the goods yard. My father immediately 'pricked up his ears' and said to me. "Tell me about kicking the football again." So I told him about the railway men kicking the football with the other blokes. Then my father said with what I detected as some satisfaction in his voice; "Don't worry son, I am going to write a letter to the railways." He did, and very shortly we had another letter telling us the charge had been dropped. That was of course a wonderful relief for both of us and I thanked him profusely. If it had been the present day I am sure that I would have given him a great big hug, but as I write this I give him one very big hug posthumously. My father finished up his working life as the credit manager of Cox Brothers, but I am sure he would have made a great lawyer. I quickly sent off an application to become an apprentice with the VR in the trade of fitting and turning. The application information brochure described each trade, and turning and fitting seemed to me to be the most interesting and practical trade of all those described. To become an apprentice in the railways in those days the applicant was required to face a selection panel, as there were too many applicants for the available positions. I was really under the height required to become an apprentice, however I hoped that my hobby of model trains might work to my advantage. By the time the day for the interview came around in November, I had at last finished my Z van and it was running around happily behind our locomotive on the layout. My father suggested that I should take along the Z van to the interview to show the panel, and of course I agreed with his suggestion to show them my work and interest in railways On the morning of the interview I dressed up in my best clothes and with my Z van in a box, I set off in the train to the Flinders Street Station, with its famous clocks at the entrance to the station. I had directions from the VR letter about the location of the room where the interview was to be held, which was in a room in the large row of buildings along the Flinders Street station complex, I quickly found the room after asking some directions from a porter and sat with a couple of other young lads until my name was called. I entered the room where the interviewing panel sat at a table, which as I remember consisted of about four men. They asked me a series of questions, and I was able to answer competently. I then passed the model over to them which they examined in detail and seemed to be very impressed, especially with its folding tail discs, I thanked them and that was it, no problem.

Flinders Street Station

Model Z guards van

A short time later I got a letter in the mail telling me that my application to become an apprentice fitter and turner, with the VR was successful, and to report to the VR Railways Head Office in Spencer Street at 10 a.m. on 10th January 1944. The family were thrilled, especially my father and if we had not been a teetotal, Christian family, I am sure that a bottle of champagne would have been opened to celebrate.

The year 1943 had been a wonderful year for me, mostly because next year I was going to begin work in the VR. As well my railway layout was a source of pure joy and being a Rover Scout was opening up an outdoor life in the mountains, which was another of my passions. It was on one of the Rover Scout hikes that my longtime friend Harry Gilham told me that he too had applied to be an apprentice coppersmith in the VR and that he too had been successful, so we would be seeing each other at Newport when we began our apprenticeships in January. That was great news. I could hardly wait for the day to come when I would begin working as a Victorian Railways apprentice fitter and turner.

CHAPTER 7

MY YEAR ONE APPRENTICESHIP BEGINS 1944-1949

On January 10th 1944, the first day of my working life began. Dressed in my second best clothes, but never the less looking spic and span, I caught the train at Rosanna to take me to Spencer Street. It was a beautiful morning, although of course I had no recollection of what the weather was really like, but even if it had been thunder and lightning with torrents of rain falling from the sky, it still would still have been a beautiful morning. I walked along Spencer Street from Spencer Street station to the Victorian Railways head office, a huge, bluestone building. I was a little early for my 10 a.m. appointment to sign up as an apprentice and so were many other young lads who were there for the same reason as me, to begin apprenticeships.

VR Head Office Spencer Street now the aptly named Grand Hotel

I had a word with a few of them as we waited on the footpath outside the building where I saw Harry Gilham. We had a short conversation before we entered the building just before 10 a.m. and found the room where we were to report. The inside of the building was as magnificent as the outside. The stairs, passages, rooms and all the fittings were constructed of beautiful brown, timbers. We were invited into a large room where a man behind a large desk, introduced himself and welcomed us to the Victorian Railways. I don't remember what his name was, but he began to call out our names. Harry was called long before me probably because his name began with a G.

When my name was called out I was ushered into a large room where I was asked a few questions and then I was directed to another room for a medical check, the first one I think I had ever had. I was asked to strip to my singlet and underpants and I was tested around my chest and back with a very cold stethoscope. Next the inside of my ears were examined with a blunt nosed, instrument and then the medical officer with a look of complete disinterest, took hold of my penis and asked me to cough. I did not know what to think I was so embarrassed. After that rather uncomfortable eexperience, I was told to dress, and then taken to a room where I had various eye sight tests, the recognition of letters and numbers, various colours, red, green, yellow and discerning forms in scrambled backgrounds. That thankfully was the last of the medical checks. I discovered later that the penis-cough test was to determine if I had a hernia, but how I never knew. It appeared that my health was OK, because nothing was said to the contrary.

I was then taken to a room with some other apprentices, where a youngish man in a blue suit introduced himself to us. "Welcome, my name is Roy Curtis, I am the Apprentice Master and I will be looking after you all during the five years of your apprenticeship. You are all to meet me at 7.30 a.m. tomorrow morning in the Administration building at the Newport Workshops. You will be able to catch a Newport Workshops train at Flinders Street Station direct to the workshops, and my office is in the brick building just across from the Newport Workshops platform." He went on to say we would need a pair of overalls and strong boots or shoes. He also gave us a plan of the workshops and vouchers that he said would give us half fare on the railways from our home station to the Newport Workshops. "I look forward to seeing you all tomorrow at 7.30 a.m. thank you." It was nearly noon when I left the building and walked back up to Spencer Street station and caught a train to Flinders Street then one back to Rosanna.

I told my parents all about the medical checkup and that I had to report to the Administration building at 7.30 a.m. the following morning at the Newport workshops. I showed my parents the voucher for my half fare railway ticket, and told them that I had to have a pair of strong boots and overalls. That was no problem as I already had a good pair of thick, black shoes and a pair of grey overalls, which I said would do until I saw what the other workers and apprentices were wearing. My father suggested that we should go down to the Rosanna station to look up the timetables and see what train I would have to catch to be at Newport by 7.30 a.m. We found there was not much choice; it would have be the 6.10 a.m.

As I presented the voucher to the porter to get my rail ticket, my father suggested that I get a yearly *first class* ticket, so that is what I asked for. "A yearly first class ticket to Newport Workshops please." Once again my father's advice was the best, because that was one of the best money saving purchases of anything I ever made, quite apart from the fact that it was a half-fare discount. The ticket if I remember cost more than my first week's wages, but that didn't matter because my father loaned me the money.

The ticket was valid seven days a week for the full year and that was really good, because I would never have to pay for another ticket when I travelled on our line and in first class too. I realized also that I would be able to use it when we went to the football at

Footscray. After tea I had a hot bath and went straight to bed in my sleep out, but not before setting the alarm for 5.30 a.m.

The alarm woke me at 5.30 a.m. and I hurriedly got up and dressed in casual clothes. By the time I made it to the kitchen, my mother was already there with my breakfast of Creamoata, a tasty and warming oats serial, served with hot milk. Not only that, but she had made a cut lunch for me too. I thanked her and said to her. "I can get my own breakfast in future thanks mum," or words to that effect. I kissed my mother goodbye and said goodbye to my father who was still in bed and he wished me a sleepy good luck. It was a lovely summer's morning and a great day to start my railway career. I walked swiftly down the road to the station in plenty of time for the train, with my overalls and lunch in a large, brown paper bag. As soon as the train came to a halt I opened the swing door and entered a new world of first class railway travel. I had never travelled first class before and the compartment was luxurious. The seats were upholstered in beautiful, green leather, at least I think it was, with loose cushions and green padded arm rests on the sides of the windows. What's more all the windows were able to be opened by means of a shiny chrome latch to whatever opening I chose. It was such a difference from travelling in second class with their hard, brown, padded seats, some even had wooden seats.

A swing door suburban train

Not only that, but many second class carriages had the electric traction motors and their gearboxes, compressors and other ancillary equipment attached to frames beneath the carriage. Many times when I travelled in a second class carriage I could feel the rumbling of the compressor and the gears of the traction motors grinding beneath my seat, especially when the train was starting and picking up speed.

This compared to the first class carriages, which were all trailers with no motors and very little ancillary gear carried beneath the carriage, made them very quiet and smooth running. I thought that without doubt, I am really going to enjoy five years of travel to the Newport Workshops each day. These swing door trains were also referred to as 'dog boxes.' The train took about thirty minutes to get to Princes Bridge Station. Leaving Princes Bridge station I walked down the ramp and along number one platform and under the subway to get to the correct platform of Flinders Street station to catch the Newport Workshops train.

A Tait suburban train

Very soon the train arrived and I got into a first class carriage, but what a difference the compartments of these carriages were to the swing door carriages. The Newport Workshops train consisted of Tait carriages, with sliding doors and short, internal passageways between the compartments. Besides that only some windows opened. Nor was the upholstery of these Tait carriages anywhere near as plush as the swing door carriages. However, I settled down to a ride in the sparsely filled carriage, which I surmised was not surprising for a train traveling through a working class district at this time of the morning.

I settled down for the journey through Footscray, Yarraville and Spotswood and after a journey of about twenty minutes, the train pulled up at the Newport Workshops open air, station platform directly opposite the Administration building. Leaving the train I gathered with a few other young blokes in front of the building where I saw Harry Gilham. I had a few words with him before we were soon all called into the office where we met Mr. Curtis the Apprentice Master. He welcomed us and read off our names to make sure no apprentice was missing and of course there wasn't. He gave us a short talk telling us that next week we would be beginning three years of instruction at the Victorian Railways Technical College at Newport, that we would be paid fortnightly, the hours of work would be 7.30 a.m. until 4.48 p.m. a 44 hour week. Our wage would be nineteen shillings (19/-) a week for the first year of our apprenticeships, and would be increased each year. He went on to say that we could catch trains each day at Flinders Street Station that would terminate at the workshops before starting time, and trains would leave the workshop's platform to go to Flinders Street after knock off time each day. Finally he said, we would get a note during the week informing us of the times and days when we would be required to attend the College.

    Mr. Curtis then directed us one by one to various workshops. I parted with Harry Gilham and together with two others apprentices I was told to walk over to the erecting shop beside the Williamstown railway line and report to the Senior Foreman Mr. Senior. It was quite a walk before we came to the erecting shop, a huge, high, long building with a saw tooth roof. We walked through a line of locomotives in various stages of repairs and I was in awe of everything I saw around me. We were directed by a bloke working on a locomotive where to find Mr. Senior, who was located in an office on one side of the building. He checked our names and gave us a numbered brass disc with a small hole in it, and if my memory serves me correctly, it was number 74. Mr. Senior told us that this was to be put on the big board when we knocked off at the end of work and picked up again in the morning.

Finally he showed us some open lockers where we could hang our clothes and leave our belongings. He then took each of us to meet the fitters we would be working with. I was taken across a couple of bays to the side of a locomotive, a class that I had never seen on our railways and introduced me to Vic King, a pleasant faced young bloke about 25 years of age. We shook hands and Vic told me to go and get into my overalls and come back and he would explain to me all about the job, the erecting shop and the locomotive. I got into my overalls and went back to Vic.

Vic explained that he was working on this Garratt the second Garratt that Vic had worked on, the first G1 having been completed in September last year in only four months, a marvellous achievement. I told him that I knew what a Garratt locomotive was as I read about them in railway books. Next he showed me how to book on a job and took me to a sound proofed, grey, telephone box, where he said to pick up the phone and when the lady answered, I was to say. "Apprentice Gordon Smith on 337," (the Garratt job number), which Vic gave me to quote. He said everything had a job number and if I changed jobs that job would have another number and I would say. "Gordon Smith, off 337 on 420," or whatever the new job number was.

Having sorted that out as we walked back to the Garratt, I was thrilled to see the *Spirit of Progress* locomotive *Sir Thomas Mitchell* in its glorious, blue and gold striped, streamlining standing on the rails of the next bay. The Garratt was in two sections, the forward unit with the driving wheels, motion gear (steam valve gear) and the water tank facing one way and behind it was an another unit, but with a coal bunker and a small water tank above its wheels and motion gear. The valve gear Vic said was called Walschaerts and he was working on each of the four sets of valve gears of this locomotive. He said the boiler was in the boiler shop and he would take me to see that later on. Vic said the Garratt was a war effort project, initiated by the authorities that found there was a need for a number of powerful locomotives to work on 3' 6" narrow gauge railways in Australia. There were 65 Garratts to be built of exactly the same design, ten in the Newport Workshops, and the remainder in other workshops around Australia.

A Queensland Railways 3' 6" gauge 4-8-2 2-8-4- Garratt
Photo QR

The pits and rails of each bay in the erecting shop were 5' 3" gauge and to accommodate the smaller gauge of the Garratts during their construction, temporary 3'6" gauge sets of rails were installed in the pits and our Garratt was standing on these. I helped Vic work on the motion gear, the term used to describe the connecting and coupling rods that connect the driving wheels together and the wheels to the cylinder through the crosshead. Vic said he had only been a tradesman fitter and turner for two years and he lived in Clayton on the Dandenong line. Vic rolled his own cigarettes in a way that I had never seen done before or since. In the top pocket of his brown, bib and brace overalls, he carried a supply of wadding. He put a small piece of this in the top of the cigarette as he rolled it to make a filter cigarette. Very clever I thought.

Lunchtime came around and I climbed up into the cab of *Sir Thomas Mitchell* and sat in the driver's seat. How thrilling I thought it must be, to be in control of one of these powerful, streamlined locomotives hauling the magnificent, long, blue and gold, striped carriages of *The Spirit* behind it. I studied all the various controls in the cab, many of which I knew their names and functions, the regulator, reversing wheel, water gauge glasses, brake controls and pressure gauges. There were a few that I was not familiar with, but I am sure I would know all about them soon.

After lunch I helped Vic assemble and adjust the clearance between the crosshead and crosshead guides (also referred to as slide bars), checking the gap with a set of feeler gauges, a new tool that I had not seen before. Thin strips of steel of various thickness in thousands of an inch, from 1/1000" to 25/1000." Vic noted down the measurement he had taken and I helped him slacken off the bolts holding the guides together, and then using the a micrometer, an accurate measuring gauge, he showed me how to hold it and measure the sizes of the thin strips of steel until he found some of the correct thickness. He placed these between the guides and the crosshead and I helped him bolt them tightly together. He then checked the clearance again with his feeler gauges to make sure it was correct, which it was.

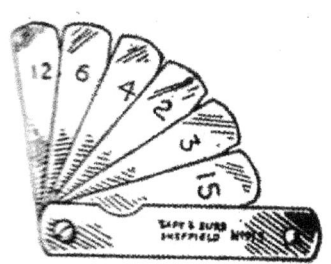

A set of feeler gauges
Photo Ken Arnold

Vic took me to the store and introduced me to the storeman named Harry and asked him for some cotton waste, which the storeman handed over to me. Vic said he would be away for a while, but to go back and give the vice a bit of a clean. I returned to the vice, a big vice sometimes referred to as an engineer's or leg vice that is opened and closed with a scissors like action by means of a long handle, to a width between the jaws of about six inches. It was the largest vice I had ever seen and it was just another one of the many new tools I had seen on my first day. Vic showed me where some kerosene was to help me clan the vice. I gave the vice a thorough cleaning and then swung the long, handle around quickly to begin closing it. This however, had a very unfortunate result for me, because the large knob at the end of the handle hit me on the head and I went 'down for the count.' Vic arrived back to find me lying limply over the vice. I had obviously been concussed and Vic, without me knowing much about how it happened, got me over to the medical centre in the workshops where I came to my senses. A nurse asked me lots of questions, took my pulse and gave me some tablets and a drink of water. I had a big lump on my head, and was made to lie down for about two hours, after which the nurse got me up and asked. "Could walk alright?" Having satisfied herself that I was alright, she said I could go back to the workshop, but to take it easy. I walked slowly back and Vic was very pleased to see I was OK. He said there was not long to knock off time, so to just sit on the bench until it's time to go.

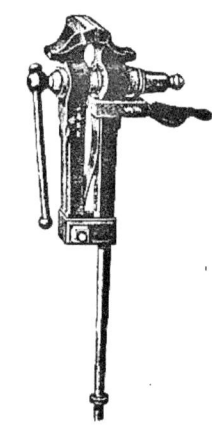

An engineer's or leg vice
photo Ken Arnold

The whistle soon sounded and I said goodbye to Vic, hung my numbered disc on the numbered hook and walked across to the train. I was home by about 5.45 p.m., where my parents were eagerly waiting to hear about my first day at the Newport Workshops. They were incredulous when I told them all about getting knocked out. My mother straight away got me a big glass of milk and told me to lie down until tea time and I did, although I felt OK. What a sad beginning to my career in the railways it was. I just hoped that the first day of my next new venture, whatever that might be, would not see me knocked out cold again, as I was on my first night in the Scouts.

The next morning when I got up my mother was already in the kitchen with a steaming plate of Creamoata on the table and my cut lunch alongside. I said to her. "Mum you don't need to get up for me, I can look after myself." I don't think she answered me, but from that for the five years I was apprenticed. I caught the 6.10 a.m. train as I would for the next five years, only missing it on very few occasions.

The author's mother Jeanie a wonderful lady

On the way across to platform six to catch the Newport Workshops train I met Harry Gilham and another of my friends from the Heidelberg State School and Scouts, Kevin Humphries, a short, freckled, red head. They naturally expected I would join them for the journey to Newport, and I did, but they entered a second class carriage when the train arrived–so what could I do, but follow. It was a Tait train as they all were on this line. The second class compartments had rather hard, brown, upholstery; otherwise the layout was the same as first class. We talked about our experiences in our new jobs and I found that Kevin had been travelling on this line for a couple of years, as he worked with the Vacuum Oil Company in Yarraville, where he got off.

Harry told me that Kevin's father Alec was a boilermaker and worked in the workshops in the boiler shop. Harry said he met him yesterday when he began work there as a coppersmith. I told Harry how I got knocked out yesterday. He couldn't believe it and said he remembered my first night in the Scouts when I got knocked out. We had a joke about it at my expense and parted when the train pulled into the workshops. I walked over to the erecting shop and picked up my tag from the board. Vic saw me and asked how I was and I said OK. The whistle sounded and we began work again on the Garratt's motion gear.

After morning tea Vic took me a tour of the workshops. He took me through the 140 yard (128 m) long erecting shop, where down the far end I saw A² and C class locomotives, and an Na class narrow gauge locomotive all in various stages of repair. At the rear of the erecting shop there was a small blacksmith's shop with a hot fire burning and a bloke working on a red hot piece of steel. Between the erecting shop and the next big building the boiler shop, there was a long open grassy space with railway tracks running between the two shops. We entered the boiler shop to be greeted by a cacophony of noise from rivet guns, hammers and I knew not what else. The boiler shop was of similar construction to the erecting shop, with a high, saw tooth roof. Inside there were boilers in various stages of repair and construction some just the bare boilers showing all the rivets and stays, some complete with smokebox and firebox, but without any cladding. Vic explained that a locomotive boiler is made up of three main sections. The firebox where the fuel is burnt, the boiler where the water is boiled to produce steam and the smokebox where the steam is exhausted to the atmosphere through the chimney, after having done its work to drive the locomotive. I didn't tell Vic I knew all about that as I felt he would think I was a 'know all' and not tell me anything more.

A scene inside the boiler shop
Drawing courtesy of Arthur Spertalis Fine Art

Vic took me over to the side of the shop where he showed me the boiler of our Garratt painted in black looking nearly complete, which was sitting on stands bearing the number G2. Alongside was another Garratt boiler still with all its rivets and stays showing, which Vic said, was the boiler for the next Garratt. At the far end of the shop a boiler, complete with smokebox and firebox was suspended vertically by an overhead crane and boilermakers were working inside the smokebox. The height of this part of the boiler shop saw tooth roof, was very high, Vic thought it was a little over 100 feet (30 m) high. We then left the boiler shop, which I had found to be really fascinating, but very noisy.

We walked back to the erecting shop and then Vic took me across another two bays of rails and pits to where there were other locomotives and parts of locomotives, frames, wheels and some boilers without cladding on frames, all very interesting to my eyes. Past these two bays we came to a machine shop, a large extension to the erecting shop with a low saw tooth roof. Vic showed me where large presses were used to press driving wheels on to their axles and I watched fascinated while this operation took place. Vic said that the diameter of the axle was slightly larger than the diameter of the hole in the driving wheel and once forced together, they would not be able to be separated, except by a special press similar to the one I was watching. After that extensive tour I thanked Vic and said I was amazed by how huge everything was. He said that tomorrow he would take me a tour of the rest of the workshops.

On the first day when together with two other apprentices, I walked over to the erecting shop to meet the Senior Foreman, I had not seen them again, which was not surprising considering how the first day ended for me. However, at lunch time we managed to get together and we introduced ourselves. One was a chubby, fair haired bloke, Kevin Peterson and the other a pleasant faced, handsome fellow Allan Henderson. We talked about where we came from and what we had been working on the first day. Both Allan and Kevin were working on different VR locomotives down the far end of the erecting shop. They were amazed when they heard what happened to me on my first day and were very interested to have a look at the locomotive that I was working on with Vic, so I took them over to show them. They were quite impressed that I was working on a brand new locomotive, while they were working on repairs to dirty, old locomotives. From that day on the three of us became firm friends. After lunch I went back to work with Vic on the Garratt, while on the next bay the *Sir Thomas Mitchell* was about to be taken out to the front of the shop and fired up.

The fitter working on *Sir Thomas Mitchell* was one I had not seen before. He was a short, pale faced man, an image of boiler suited, sartorial, elegance. He was attired in a clean, freshly ironed, light blue boiler suit, with a matching blue, locomotive driver's *starched* cap. He was quite a sight to behold! Vic introduced me to him. His name was Orb Pullen. We watched as a small locomotive with a hook backed on to the *Sir Thomas Mitchell* and Orb scurried around as it was coupled on, then he climbed into the cab as it was towed out to the front of the shop. Vic told me that Orb worked exclusively on the streamlined S class *Spirit* locomotives and always looked as I first saw him. Vic thought he must wash, dry and iron his boiler suit and starch his cap each night, or he must have many other caps and boiler suits to change into, which I thought was more likely. Orb he said, was involved in the theatre, although how he never told me, maybe because he didn't know. Orb I thought was eminently suited to working on the S class three cylinder, *Spirit of Progress* locomotives which at the time were the pride of the VR and were treated as such when they were being worked on in the erecting shop.

The carriage shops and clock tower

In the afternoon Vic continued with the tour, first taking me out to the front of the erecting shop where the *Sir Thomas Mitchell* was being fired up and after having a quick look, across towards the Administration building, past a row of workshops, some of which he said were where carriages were built and maintained. He said *The Spirit* carriages had been built in there. A little further along Vic pointed down a wide lane between the carriage shops and the Administration building and said that at the far end, Beaufort aeroplanes were being built, but we could not go down there as it was a prohibited area. He said the workshops were also building Bren gun carriers and that too was a prohibited area.

Moving on past the lane we came to the Administration building with its magnificent, clock tower with clocks on each of its four sides. Vic said the building was usually always referred to as the "Clock Tower." Strangely, it had not made much of an impression on me on the first day when we met Mr. Curtis there. Past the clock tower we came to a low building, which Vic said was the turnery. He took me in and we walked past many machines, but the only ones I recognised were lathes. Further in to the left he showed me a big wheel lathe that was taking a huge cut of metal from the tyre of one of a pair of large diameter, driving wheels.

The Administration building and clock tower

Leaving the turnery we walked along to another row of workshops like the carriage shop. There was an open door in one of these and taking up the whole width of the door, was the steel, stern of a ship. I could not believe my eyes. Vic said the ship was a 75 foot ocean going tug, which was being built in the workshops as another contribution towards the war effort. The tug was taking up one half of the tender shop leaving only one bay for the maintenance of tenders. The workshops had already built two of these tugs and when this one was complete; there would be another one to follow. Further along there was a foundry and a brake shop, but that was as far as we went because we had to get back to the Garratt. On the way back however, we dropped into a small workshop where wagon bearings were being fitted. In the corner was another unexpected sight, that of a large brass propeller, which was having the surfaces of its blades ground. I estimated that the propeller was about five feet in diameter. There was no doubt that Newport Workshops was doing a great lot to support the war.

We walked back to the erecting shop to the Garratt where Vic checked the clearance again between the crosshead and crosshead guides. He said it wasn't quite right, so I helped him unbolt them and select some different thickness packing pieces that he put in place and we bolted it all together again. After checking the clearance with his feeler gauges he said that at this time it was OK.

By now it was nearly knock off time and sure enough after we had a rest for a while, the whistle blew and we said goodbye to each other and off I went to catch the train. Not waiting to see if Harry was around, I climbed into a first class carriage and was soon home with no traumas to report to my parents, but telling them a little of what I did during the day, and how I was enjoying being an apprentice fitter and turner. The rest of my first week was much the same as the first couple of days, except that on the Thursday I was handed a memo informing me that I was to begin my schooling at the Victorian Railways Technical College on Monday at 12.30 p.m. to 4.30 p.m. and on Wednesdays at 8 a.m. to 12 noon. Following that I was to report to Senior Foeman Tom Harmon in the brake shop on Thursday at 7.30 a.m. It all sounded very interesting and before long Allan and Kevin came to see me to see if I had got the same note as them. We compared memos with the result that we would all be together, which made us very happy.

Vic said that I would find my time at the College very interesting and that I would be going there for the next three years, but did not say much about me having to report to Tom Harmon in the brake shop except to say, I would be learning a lot about fitting. My first week finally came to an end and I told my parents about having to go to the Victorian Railways Technical College next week and that it was a three year course. This set my father thinking and he said to me. "Why don't I think of going one night a week back to the RMTC to study one of the subjects you missed out on?" I gave this some thought and said that I would see what it involved and make a decision before night school began at the end of January. I finally decided that yes, I would take my father's suggestion.

CHAPTER 8

THE WAR, THE GARRATT AND TWO COLLEGES 1944

Suddenly, it was the last week in January and time for our family holiday at Edithvale, and on the Saturday our family were off to Edithvale. It was a new experience for me as I had to travel to the Newport workshops from there. I went to the Edithvale station, but I no longer had my VR voucher to get half fare, however I showed my ticket to the station master and he gave me a weekly concession ticket to Flinders Street. "First Class?" he asked. "No, second class," I replied, as there was no way I was going to pay extra for the dubious extra comfort of a first class Tait compartment.

I travelled from Edithvale each morning, only changing into first class when I changed into the Newport Workshops train at Flinders Street. For the next two weeks I had to catch a train from Edithvale a little earlier than from Rosanna to get me to Newport in time. My mother was still getting me up with breakfast and a cut lunch each day, even though she was on holiday. I protested, but to no avail. I didn't see much of the beach except before tea when I went down for a swim and of course on the weekends. I bought another weekly ticket for the next week at the same concession and soon traveling to work from Edithvale was over until next year.

I continued on with Vic working on the Garratt, then one day another *Spirit* locomotive, *Edward Henty* was pushed into the bay beside us. Orb in his clean, well pressed, overalls got to work dismantling the blue and yellow striped panels from the sides of the S class, which were then wrapped in thick hessian covers. Snow our rigger hooked them up with the lifting tackle, chains as I remember, and lifted them over to the side of the shop where they were carefully stored. The front, streamlined doors with the gold, VR winged crests, were taken off with great care by Orb, and these too, as with all the streamlining on the locomotive were wrapped in hessian and carefully put in storage with the rest of the panels.

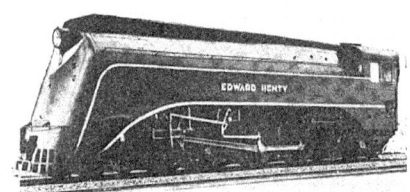

S class 4-6-0 Edward Henty
Photo VRPP

Except in photographs I had never seen what an S class locomotive looked like before it was streamlined and now even in this stripped condition with all the streamlining panels taken off the three cylinder locomotive with its Walschaerts valve gear was a sleek looking locomotive. I watched as Orb, together with a couple of other not so immaculately attired fitters during the following day, dismantled the motion gear and each part was taken away to be examined and overhauled. Such work as the re-metalling and machining of the coupling and connecting rod bearings and other work would be carried out as required. All locomotives from the most highly celebrated classes like the S and H classes to the lowest E and Y classes, not forgetting the narrow gauge locomotives, all had to undergo periodic examinations and overhauls based mostly on mileage as shown below.

'A' every 1,500 miles
'AB' every 3,000 miles
'ABC' every 12,000 miles
'ABCD' every 24,000 miles

The S class came in for much shorter periodic inspections than other locomotives due to their importance as the modern image of the VR, Besides there were only four of them to keep *The Spirit* running every day. Al of these overhauls and examinations were scheduled to take various lengths of time and there was a detailed list of components for each that had to be attended to in some manner, repaired or replaced. Newport Workshops carried out most of the major examinations, leaving the others to railway workshops in

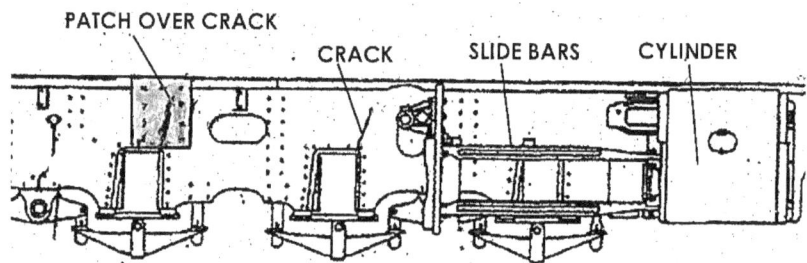

A typical locomotive plate frame showing the location of a crack and patch

North Melbourne, Ballarat, Bendigo and other regional workshops and running sheds. Walking around the workshop for the first time by myself, I saw many interesting maintenance jobs taking place on a couple of locomotive classes. An A^2 class was having a patch riveted to its frame cover a crack that originated in the gap in the frame where the horn guides holding the wheels in place are located. It was fascinating watching the rivets being heated to a glowing red heat in a small brazier. The red hot rivet was then quickly handed up with a pair of tongs to a boilermaker working from inside the frame, who placed the red hot rivet, in a hole in the frame and held it there firmly, while the rivet was capped with a pneumatic hammer by another boilermaker on the outside of the frame, both of whom as I remember, were not wearing ear or eye protection, and that together with the general noise level I was subjected to in the erecting shop over the years, contributed to the hearing loss I now have. During my time in the erecting shop, I saw locomotives other than A^2s having patches put on in the same area around the horn section. This appeared to be a weak part in a plate frame. At least the riveting of the patch did not have to be waterproof as they did on riveted ships like the *Titanic*. There was an X class 2-8-2 'Mikado' in the shop on jacks, which enabled me to see the booster of the X class that I could not see when I was lucky enough to see an X class on the way home from the football, because the booster is hidden inside the trailing truck, so at last I was going to be able to see this wonderful piece of machinery. The booster engine-trailing truck assembly was separated from the X, and was lying across the pit behind it. It was very dirty, but I was able to see the outline of the little, two cylinder, steam engine that through a system of cranks and gears, provided the X class with extra power (tractive effort), for starting and at slow speeds. The X class as I like to describe it is a locomotive with the appearance of powerful beauty. It was the most powerful locomotive on the VR and was used as a goods locomotive until the more powerful H class came along.

A Booster as fitted to an X class

Vic said to go and have a look at the boiler of a K class that was about to be lifted off its frames and wheels, so I walked across to have a look at this new sight. The K class with its cab removed, had a thick wire hawser placed around its smoke box, and a strong, steel, L shaped hook, inserted in the fire box door. Both were connected to the hooks of each of the overhead travelling cranes. On a signal from Snow, both cranes in unison silently and slowly lifted the boiler from the frames, as fitters on the floor made sure that it was lifted free of any obstruction within the frames. Clear of the frame and lifted high above it, on a signal from Snow, both cranes made a pleasant grinding sound, as together they began moving the boiler down to the far end of the erecting shop towards the boiler shop. I was to see this sight over and over again with many different locomotives, but this first lift was an awesome sight, although I loved watching every big lift that I could see, but especially those when a complete locomotive was lifted. The K class 2-8-0 'Consolidation' was a very versatile locomotive that was able to operate over nearly all the VR lines, both main and branch lines, hauling passenger, mixed and goods trains. I would describe it as a locomotive with compact power. There are also a couple of K class locomotives still being operated by heritage organisations in Victoria at the time of writing.

A K class 2-8-0 'consolidation' locomotive
photo VRCEPP

The war news was all about the Allies landing in Anzio in Central Italy and how they were involved in heavy fighting as they pushed to the north against the Germans, but my main interest apart from the war news was running trains on my layout, while weekends would usually find me on hiking trips with the Rover Scouts, I began work with Vic on Monday morning on the crosshead and guides of the Garratt on the other side of the front unit. I had to go to the store on a few occasion for various tools and was startled by the store man's actions as he didn't seem to be able to keep still. I mentioned this to Vic who he said that Harry had a condition called 'Saint Vitus's Dance' a disorder of the nervous system, which made him unable to control his arms and legs, but he was able to do a good job as a store man, just ignore it and you will get used to him. Some called him 'Harry hopper,' but of course not to his face.

In the high roof above the erecting shop there were three large travelling cranes, two 75 ton and one 20 ton. The 20 ton crane was always busy transferring bits and pieces of locomotives around the shop. Vic introduced me to a fair haired bloke in overalls he called 'Snow.' I had seen him attach the hook and chains from the crane on to items to be lifted and using hand signals, direct the crane driver sitting in a cabin above to lift the load and move it to where it was to go. Vic said Snow was a rigger (sometimes called a floor man) who had done a training course in rigging, learning everything about lifting tackle, chains, ropes, wires and their lifting capacities. They learned the correct way to use these, and Vic thought the course took about six months, after which Snow was awarded a Crane Floor Man's Certificate. It was not a trade as such, but at the time of writing, it certainly is. There are many categories of this trade now, because of the variety of jobs where a large number of types of large and small cranes are used in buildings and construction projects in Australia and around the world.

I spent the morning working on the Garratt and just before noon, Vic said that on school days I was allowed to leave ten minutes before lunch time at 12 noon, to allow me to walk the quarter of a mile up to the College. He said I did not need to book off the Garratt as the job clerks were notified when each of the apprentices attended college and the brake shop. He asked me for my disc and said he has the OK to put it on the board when he knocked off. After Vic took care of my disc on that first day, I have absolutely no recollection of how my disc was managed when I went to college and the brake shop, because it always seemed to be there for me when I began work each morning.

When the time came for me to leave I put my overalls away, washed my hands and began walking up the path to the College. As I walked along I could hear a lot of noise coming from the other side of the Williamstown railway line where there was a large railway marshalling yard that I had not noticed before. The noise was coming from an E class 0-6-0 T tank shunting locomotive that was fly shunting wagons that were rolling along a slight downgrade and colliding with great force and noise into the buffers of the wagons on the same siding. This yard was where goods trains were being assembled. I ate my sandwiches and very soon I was joined by Kevin and Allan and some other blokes waiting for the time to go into the College. Harry Gilham had told me that because his trade as a coppersmith involved some different subjects than mine, he would not be going to College on the same days and times as me.

By 12.30 p.m. there were about eight blokes there when the time came to enter the front door, where we were met by a middle aged man who directed us in to a classroom. He said his name was Mr. Grace and he welcomed us into the College and into the big family of the Victorian Railways. He said that we will be attending the College twice each week for the first three years of our five year apprenticeship. Then one by one our names and trades were called out. As well as we three fitters and turners, there were a couple of interlocking fitters, three boiler makers and one weighbridge fitter. Mr. Grace told us that "All the subjects that you will be studying here will have a special reference to the railways, and will help you in the learning of your trade in the workshop. All of you here today will be together for the first year and the subjects you will be learning are applicable to the trades that you represent."

He then introduced us to a Mr. Hendrick saying. "Mr. Hendrick will be with you in this class room this afternoon and will be instructing you in the subject of Geometry." There were nine of us in the class and we sat at wooden desks. The classroom had a small raised platform with a large blackboard on the wall behind. We were issued with notes and Mr. Hendrick described various simple shapes and some calculations regarding each shape.

At 4.30 p.m. the class ended and we all filed out of the class room at the end of what appeared to me as the beginning of three years of enjoyable learning. First indications were that it was not going to be too difficult, particularly considering the time and subjects that I had studied at the RMTC. Whether their records of my previous schooling contained this information I never knew. Kevin lived in Newport so he just walked home, while I went with Allan to the station across the road and caught the train to Flinders Street. I was very happy to discover that we both walked towards a first class carriage that Allan travelled first class too. He said: "Why not, its half price, cheap and the seats are more comfortable?" When we arrived at Flinders Street station, Allan said he lived in Sandringham, so we parted.

I went across to Princess Bridge station, where I saw a shunting operation that I had seen a few times previously. During off peak periods the usual seven car train was split in two, three carriages were taken off and stored in the Jolimont yards, and then in the peak periods the three carriages were brought back and coupled back up to make a seven carriage train again. I was standing on the platform waiting to board the train, but was not allowed until the connection had been made. The three carriages were slowly driven back under the shunter's signals and brought gently into buffer contact. As I watched, the shunter with gloved hands climbed down and coupled the two sections together with the screw link coupling and adjusted the slack with the coupling's handle. Then after connecting the brake hoses and electrical cables he climbed back up on to the platform. The passengers were then allowed to board. I got home a bit earlier and told my parents and brothers about my first day at the Victorian Railways Technical College, the 'College' for short, which they all thought was going to be very good for me. My parents thought that it might be a good idea to try and complete the certificate course at the RMIT. Although my memory of that first day at the College is fairly clear, my memory of the following three years at 98 years of age has allowed me to write this second edition.

The next day Vic asked me how I went at College and I told him all about it. He said that he enjoyed his time there and he reckoned I would too. The next couple of days passed working on the Garratt, which was getting very close to completion. Having adjusted the four sets of crosshead and guide clearances, the next job Vic said was to adjust the valve settings. After work I went up to the RMIT and ended up enrolling in Applied Mechanics, the subject I had failed in and which I thought would be the best to pass as being somewhat relevant to my future railway career. The class was on a Wednesday night from 5.30 p.m. to 8.30 p.m. and classes began on the first week in February. My father was very pleased with my decision.

On Wednesday morning I was able to catch a later train and travelled as usual in superlative comfort, this time with a few more passengers in the compartment until I got to Princess Bridge station. Many times on the 6.10 a.m. train I was the sole occupant of a compartment all the way to Princes Bridge. Then as always I travelled in the less than superlative, Tait first class carriage to Newport station, where I crossed over Melbourne Road to the College past the railway gates that very rarely seemed to be open for the passage of road transport, not that there was much of it in those days anyway.

In contrast to the road traffic, there was nearly a continuous movement of trains of all descriptions travelling to and fro over the crossing. I met Kevin and Allan and the other members of the class and we began a new subject 'Heat Engines', exactly the same name as the subject I studied and passed at the RMIT. With the help of some slides projected on to the wall; the history of the steam engine was traced from its beginning with emphasis on the advent of the first steam locomotives.

Walking back to the workshops with Kevin and Allan, Kevin told us that our college was referred to as 'Bonehead College' or simply 'bonehead,' and that this had been its nickname for many years. We thought that was quite amusing, although as I was to discover, it was not because the subjects taught there were brainless, or we who studied there were in the same category, it actually came to be a term of endearment. I will however refer to it as 'College' in this book. Having digested that interesting bit of information, we paused for a while to watch all the shunting activity taking place. As the fly shunted wagons collided, the noise of the crash was very loud and raised dust from some of the wagons. We wondered if any of the wagons held goods and if they did how they avoided damage. Kevin said that tank wagons were not allowed to be fly shunted, which we thought was a very sensible regulation. This was the early years of the beginning of the transition from three link couplings to automatic couplings.

It was very interesting watching the shunters in their blue suits and wide, brim hats, using a long pole to uncouple the wagons attached to the shunting engine, to free them before they were given a push down to the correct siding. This most times it needed another shunter to hold open the point lever or change the points as the wagons passed by. When the goods train had been finally put together, the shunters had to go along and couple them up with three link non-screw couplings and connect all the brake hoses. A shunter's job must keep them very fit I thought, but it was also a very dangerous job where a shunter must always be very conscious of the dangers around him.

This was a much harder shunting job than I had seen happen on Princess Bridge station last Monday with the suburban train. Allan said he wanted to get a locomotive driver's cap and we all thought that was a good idea as many blokes in the erecting shop wore them, although Vic didn't. The cap was made of soft, navy blue, material with a small peak, so we decided to enquire where we could buy them.

Back on the Garratt, the next job after the crosshead and guide clearances were complete, was to set the valve travels. Locomotive valve gears control the admission of steam into the cylinders of the locomotive, and in doing this are designed to perform a number of functions. Move the locomotive forward or reverse, adjust the 'cut off' of the steam at some point during the full travel of the piston, to provide the most economic use of steam and the efficient running of a locomotive under all operating conditions.

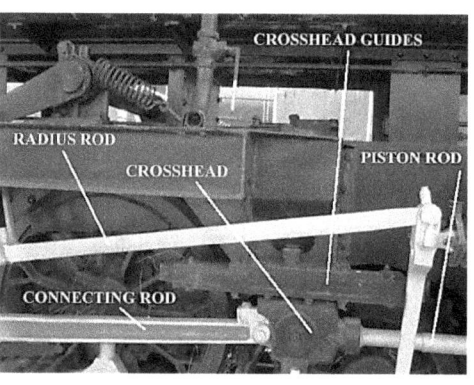

A photo showing some components of the motion and valve gear of the Garratt

The driver has full control of these functions by use of the reversing wheel or lever. There are two main types of valve gear used on the VR. Walschaerts valve gear, which is fitted to the most recently built classes of locomotives running on the VR. This valve gear consists of a system of cranks, bars, rods and links connected on the outside of the driving wheels. Stephenson's valve gear is another type of valve gear also using a system of rods and links, but the connection to the valve is by eccentrics attached to a driving wheel axle between the frames of the locomotive, and so is not visible from outside the locomotive. Stephenson's valve gear is not as versatile as Walschaerts and not as easy to service, but early $A2^2$s and many other VR locomotives were fitted with this valve gear. There were other forms of valve gear used on VR locomotives.

I learned later that the conjugating gear fitted on the S class *Spirit* locomotives, to control the admission of steam into their centre, third cylinders, was found to be were very difficult to maintain. When the H class with its third cylinder was designed, a simplified version of this gear form called the 'Gresley' conjugating gear was fitted to the third, centre cylinder of the H class, and to my knowledge caused no problems. The famous *Flying Scotsman* locomotives of the LNER in the UK had Gresley valve gear, and they ran hundreds of miles each day between London and Edinborough.

To set the valve gear on the Garratt (four sets), the locomotive had to be moved backwards and forwards on the rails to find the extreme ends of the travel of the pistons in the cylinders. The two sets of driving wheels, those under the water tank and the coal tender were not joined together at this time; they would only be joined together when the boiler was installed, so each set had to be moved separately. The method of moving the Garratt and other locomotives for this work was by means of pinch bars, long, steel bars with one end tapered to a chisel point and turned up slightly. These bars were inserted under some of the driving wheels of the Garratt, and used to move the Garratt backwards and forwards very small distances as required. To man the pinch bars a few fitters and labourers were taken from other jobs they were working on.

It was then that I met another erecting shop character also called Harry. He was a labourer who slobbered a lot, wore filthy overalls and a battered, dirty felt hat, the absolute opposite of Orb Pullen's impeccable image. Besides, Harry was a little dense, but Vic said he was always used to help pinch locomotives. Harry was a source of mirth, because although he puffed and dribbled profusely as he moved the pinch bar up and down, his pinch bar many times lagged behind the movement of the locomotive. No one minded it was just the way he was, and I was pleased that even with his deficiencies the VR chose to employ him as a labourer, with a use in the industry, the same as Harry the store man.

After the extreme limits of the piston travel were found, Vic checked the valve piston travel and found it was not right, so he determined the correction needed and marked this amount on the radius rod with a centre punch. A centre punch mark is a small indentation put in a piece of metal as a reference point. It is made by a 'centre punch,' a short, steel, pencil like tool, with a hardened, point on one end and when hit with a hammer makes a 'centre pop' mark. Vic said the rod was a little too long and he would remove it and take it to the blacksmith to get him to shorten it. By this time it was knock off time and Vic, knowing that I had to go to the brake shop the following morning said there was still three more to be checked, so you will see how it is done tomorrow or the next day.

A centre punch
photo courtesy of Ken Arnold

CHAPTER 9

THE GARRATT AND THE CUBE 1944

At 7.30 a.m. the following morning I met Kevin and Allan in the brake shop a low, saw tooth, roof building occupied by men working on various jobs at the back of the building. In front of these there were a couple of rows of benches with vices attached to them, but not engineer's vices, I hasten to add. From the door of an office with glass windows a short man with black, curly hair, emerged and introduced himself to us as Mr. Harmon. He called out our names and went on to say; "You boys will be with me each Thursday morning for the next twelve months. During this time you will be learning some of the most important skills of your trade, the use of hand tools, chisels, files and scrapers. You will find that the project I am about to describe to you will be difficult at first, but will become easier as your skill increases. When you have completed the project you will be in possession of the most important, basic skills of your trades, which you will make use of in your apprenticeship and when you qualify as tradesmen."

With those opening words he took us over to one of the benches on which there were a number of cubes of metal in various worked forms. We crowded around and Mr. Harmon pointed to one cube, a 6" (15 cm) cube of dark grey, cast iron. He then pointed to the next one, which had a series of grooves cut across it. Pointing to the other cubes in turn he explained the various stages of the project and its completion. "Are there any questions?" There were no questions because I think we were all a little over-awed by the task we saw in front of us. I know I was.

Mr. Harmon asked us to pick up a cast iron cube from the side of his office and carefully take it to a bench, put it in the vice and tighten it up. The cube was very heavy and after we had all managed to do that successfully without any of us dropping it on our feet, Mr. Harmon asked us to come over to another bench where he already had a cube in a vice and said to us. "When you get back to your bench you will find a pair of safety glasses that you must wear at all times. As well you will find a sharpened ¼ inch wide crosscut chisel, a one and a half pound ball-peen hammer and a steel rule, ready there for you to use. I will now show you how to begin cutting the first groove." He then held up his hammer saying; "The correct way to hold a hammer is by the end of the handle, **NOT** halfway down the handle. Do not choke the hammer." He then put on his safety glasses and proceeded to show us how to hold the hammer and chisel making the first blows on the chisel to begin a ¼" (6 mm) deep cut in one side and end of the cube.

The cube showing where the grooves were to be cut with the crosscut chisel

He certainly knew how to use a hammer and chisel. It was amazing to see how effortless it seemed to him. After he made a groove about an inch long he stopped and turned to us all saying; "Off you go back to your benches and make a start." With the noise of hammers striking chisels all around me, and the occasional cries of "ow!" and other exclamations of anguish, some of them coming from my own lips as the hammer missed the chisel and landed on the back of my wrist. I persevered and finally got the chisel to make a nick in the side of the cube in the correct position.

After about an hour of intent toil, together with a few more knocks on my wrist, I managed to make a short groove at the correct depth and direction. I had a quick glimpse at the sample with its criss-crossing grooves, four on one side and then another four at right angles. I thought that it would take the whole five years of my apprenticeship to complete at my rate of progress. It was time for a break and as we milled around talking to each other, I could not help but notice that the wrist of one of the blokes in the class was bleeding. Kevin and Allan had been able to progress about as far with the first groove as me and said that they had hit their wrists a couple of times too. After the pause I hammered and chiseled on, as gradually, very, gradually I think, I was beginning to get the hang of it. I used the steel rule to make sure that I was chiseling in the right direction and depth, although by lunch time I had only got about halfway across the face. Mr. Harmon came around and looked at our work. He seemed to be satisfied with my progress and thankfully that was the end of the 'first day of the cube,' but there were many more such days to come.

As I walked across to the erecting shop with Kevin and Allan we consoled each other with our sore wrists, but none were bleeding. Allan said to make sure to hold the hammer at the end; because he saw Mr. Harmon knock the elbow of one apprentice who was choking the hammer and this made the hammer head land hard on his wrist. It appeared that this was Mr. Harmon's rather cruel cure for this grave error. Kevin found out that the caps we wanted to get could be bought in a shop in Newport and he was going to get one when he knocked off. Allan and I decided to go to the shop next Monday before going to College.

We left the brake shop and after lunch get back to the real world of locomotives, which for me was the Garratt. Vic asked me: "How did you get on in the brake shop?" "OK, but it was not very easy," I said. "Don't worry, it gets much easier after the first few weeks," Vic quickly assured me. For the remainder of the week I worked on the Garratt, helping Vic complete the valve measurements on the other side of the Garratt and take off the radius rod, which also had to be shortened. This he said would be done by 'jumping' the rod.

Between us we took the not too heavy rod, down to the small blacksmith's shop at the back of the erecting shop. He introduced me to the blacksmith and told him that the rod had to be shortened. While we stood there we watched the blacksmith put the centre of the rod over the red hot coke fire and heat the area where Vic had put the two centre pop marks. As soon as the rod was red hot the blacksmith held it up vertically and banged (jumped) the end down on the anvil making it shorter. Vic, using a pair of pointed, compass like dividers, checked to see if the distance was correct. It wasn't, it was still was a little too long. It took a couple of further heatings to a glowing red heat and a little more jumping, then with a few blows of a large hammer to straighten the rod, it was deemed to be the correct length. We thanked the blacksmith and took the rod back to the Garratt and fitted it between the expansion link and the combination lever.

The next week at lunch time before College, Allan and I purchased our caps, which we donned and complemented each other on our looks. The two days at school Monday morning and Wednesday afternoon were much the same as the first week, learning the same subjects in a bit more detail. Then came Thursday morning and it was off to the brake shop again and the cube. We toiled through the morning and gradually our skill swinging the hammer by the end of its handle on to the head of the chisel, and not on the back of our wrists was improving. I was very pleased with myself, only missing the chisel head or not striking it dead in the centre, only a couple of times. I had also managed to keep the depth of the groove to its correct depth and its direction parallel to the side of the cube. There were very few cries of anguish from some of the blokes who were making heavy weather of it, and had to be helped by Mr. Harmon. Some in fact had to go to the medical centre to have bloodied wrists bandaged, and there were some too that were bruised, but not bloodied. Mr. Harmon had got his point across that the hammer must not be 'strangled,' a crime that it seemed was nearly as bad as strangling a human being.

The tools used in the project L to R. Crosscut chisel-flat chisel-scraper-square-steel rule-second cut file-ball peen hammer

At the end of the second day I had completed the first groove and had begun the second. Talking with Kevin and Allan afterwards Kevin said he that had nearly finished his second groove. Part way through the morning, Mr. Harmon took us aside to a grinding wheel and showed us how to sharpen the chisel to the correct angle, warning us not to let the chisel get too hot, to keep cooling it in the water tray provided below each wheel. From then on we sharpened our own chisels. The usual weekly interruptions of College for two half days a week and the cube for another half day was frustrating, because working on the Garratt with Vic was far more interesting. Over the last few weeks of January and the first weeks of February, nearly four months after G1 was completed, our Garratt's driving units were ready to be joined to their boiler.

Sadly the lifts happened on a Thursday morning when I was in the brake shop working on the cube. By the time I got to the erecting shop after lunch, and began working again with Vic on the Garratt, the two driving units were standing on a section of the 3' 6" gauge rails at the far end of the erecting shop. Beside it was G2's boiler on a flat truck, which had been brought from the boiler shop and was ready to be lifted into position. The boiler complete with its cab and the number plate, proudly displaying G2 on the side of the cab was looking really impressive with its gloss black, coat of paint. Our driving units too had been painted in gloss black before we began working on them. During the afternoon Vic hurried around with other fitters and boilermakers as the two driving units, which had already been spotted at the correct distance apart, were ready to accept the boiler.

I couldn't wait to see it all go together and without too much delay the boiler was lifted in much the same manner as I had seen the K class lifted the other day, except that because the cab was already in place, chains were hooked on the side of the boiler beneath the firebox. A foreman I had not seen before, directed the lift in conjunction with Snow our rigger, and the boiler was gradually lowered on to its pivots, but not before one of the driving assemblies had to be pinched a little to make the connection.

Many different size pipes and hoses for steam, water and the brakes then had to be installed and connected. The live steam pipes from the smokebox to the front and back cylinders, the exhaust steam pipes back to the blast pipe and chimney, and the pipes taking water from the tender tanks to the boiler. (Some of these had already been fitted while the boiler was in the boiler shop). Next the cab controls, brakes, reversing gear, release cocks, injectors and all the other controls had to be fitted too, not forgetting the electrical connections, the wiring from the turbo generator to the headlights, marker lights and cab lights. All of this work had to be carried out and tested in the shop, before the Garratt could be fired up and moved under its own

Photos of a Garratt showing some of the pipes and hose connections

power on the set of 3'. 6" gauge of rails between the erecting shop and boiler shop.

The rest of the day I helped Vic with some of this work and soon realized that a Garratt is a much more complicated locomotive than an ordinary tender or tank locomotive, with all the pipes, hoses and other connections that have to be maintained in good working order, especially the flexible joints carrying high pressure steam to the cylinders of the rear section.

The following day while work was still going on putting all the parts of the Garratt together, Vic said he had another job for me and he took me over to a bay further over from where we had been working on the Garratt. Laid out on wooden sleepers were four large steel plates. These were the frames for the new Garratt G3, (or so I thought), the next Garratt to be built in the Newport Workshops. The frames, about ¾" (2 cm) thick had all the sections cut out for the horn guides and these large plates of steel would soon become the spines of the Garratt. The frames were also riddled with drilled holes of all sizes and my job as I was to discover, was to 'deburr' the holes of 'burrs', the word describing the sharp edges around the circumference of the holes left by the drilling machine. I had already become familiar with many new tools of my trade and I was about to discover another one. A 'deburring' tool, made out of a worn square file, which was ground at one end to produce two faces at a slight angle to make two cutting edges, then heated and bent into a curved shape at the end, and fitted with a file handle.

The tool is inserted into the hole as shown in the accompanying diagram and held firmly down while it is rotated a couple of evolutions and this action removes the burrs. This was to be my rather boring job for the next couple of days, but thankfully not all the holes in each of the four frame plates had to be deburred, not the many small rivet holes, only those holes that were to have machined bolts inserted in them to secure the various components to the frames. The burrs were sharp, so I had to take great care not to injure myself on their sharp jagged edges. Vic said to make sure to get some hessian bags to sit on as I worked, to prevent me getting 'piles' whatever that was, and to take a rest every now and again and come and have a look at the Garratt where he was working, so of course I needed no encouragement to do as he suggested.

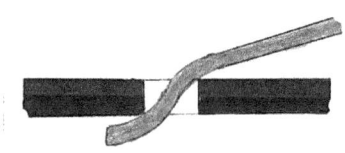

A deburring tool in use

The deburring job wasn't too hard, and after lunch I went to have a look at the Garratt. A fire had just been built in the firebox and the Garratt was doing its best to raise steam pressure. One fitter called Jim, a slim fellow who I had spoken to on a few occasions, was doing some work between the frames of the forward tank unit, which was being filled with water with a long hose. Suddenly, Jim let out a loud yell as the tank overflowed and the water ran down the sides of the tank and soaked him! Amidst a string of profanities, Jim climbed out of the frames and began to dry himself off, much to the amusement of all of us. A little later when there was some steam pressure, someone in the cab decided to blow the whistle mounted on an angle on the front of the smokebox, which caused a jet of water to be ejected from the whistle and spray some of us standing below, which caused more mirth and some more profanities. It appeared that the Garratt was not to be moved that day; the raising of steam was only to check for leaks. I went back to hole deburring and that was the end of another very interesting week as a fitting and turning apprentice.

Back to work on Monday and more deburring until Vic came and told me that the Garratt was being fired up again, so I went to the back of the erecting shop where the Garratt was building up steam. Although the Garratt did not yet have a full head of steam, as the safety valve was not blowing off, Mr. Senior the foreman climbed into the cab and opened the regulator. With the release cocks blowing noisy, jets of steam from both ends and with a low, puff, puff, puff, puff, the Garratt was coaxed slowly along the 3' 6" gauge rails between the two workshops, luckily just minutes before I was due to leave for College. It was a great and thrilling occasion for me. I was actually seeing a locomotive that I had helped to build, come to life. There appeared to be a few small leaks here and there, but nothing that destroyed the image for me of G2 a very impressive locomotive.

Kevin and Allan also came out to see the Garratt, so we all left and walked up to the College together. The Garratt was later divided into the three units and each unit was loaded on to bogie flat wagons and tied down securely before being taken away to be delivered to one of the railways designated to receive it, but I sadly did not see any of this action, because it was time to go to College. The classes at College were quite interesting and well within my ability to understand. In Heat Engines the instruction was really all about locomotives, learning about the boiler, its components, functions and its control and operation. Geometry was no trouble, and we quickly passed on from plain Geometry to Solid Geometry, with calculations concerning solid shapes and forms, cylinders, cones and how these could be made from a flat sheet of steel or other material. This was accomplished by a process called 'development,' which involved the use of drawing instruments, compasses and the like.

All the necessary drawing instruments were provided by the college and the instructors were very good and likable, some of whom I believe were former VR apprentices. On the other hand, my schooling at the RMTC was not progressing very well as I was finding it hard to stay awake, which was not surprising I suppose, having to get up each day at 5.45 a.m. however, I kept at it, but I think it was getting beyond me.

Working on the cube was beginning to become a much easier task, as I was now able to bring hammer and chisel together in a much more efficient manner with virtually no damage to my wrist. Most of the class including myself had completed the cross hatching, having chiseled away the hatched layer on the first side to reveal a fairly flat, but rough surface. The next job was to use the flat chisel with the assistance of the rule, to gradually flatten the surface. Mr. Harmon said. "The flatter you can make the surface with the flat chisel; the easier it will be to carry out the next job of using a second cut file to produce a surface ready to be scraped." Scraping was as yet an unknown quantity for me, but looking at the sample cubes I could see how very flat the surface was after it had been scraped. Getting the first side reasonably flat with the chisel was not too hard a task, but took a couple of Thursday mornings.

Back at work on the Garratt frames that I had been deburring, Vic told me they were not for G3 at all. After I had finished deburring them, they were to be taken away to become the frames of G4. In their place two sets of frames complete with the cylinders and all the wheels were brought in to us on flat trucks and the cranes lifted them on to the 3' 6" gauge rails. As I remember, these had been assembled in the tender shop, and the cylinder castings, after having been machined in the turnery, together with all the wheels were attached there.

One afternoon a red headed bloke in a boiler suit came over to where Vic and I were working and said to me: "Gordon you are to come with me and work on a job I have for you. My name is Alec Humphreys, call me Alec. You know my son Kevin. Vic knows all about this and you will be back with him soon." I followed Alec out to the front of the erecting shop where two 20 ton wrecking cranes were stabled. Alec, referring to me as Gordy, which was the name he always called me from then on, said. "Let's climb up into the cab of the crane and I'll show you what I want you to do for me." We climbed up and Alec pointed down to a series of rods where they lay under part of the crane's grease covered gears. "What I want you to do Gordy is to take these split pins and the screwdriver and get under there and put the split pins in the holes in the clevis pins."

All of a sudden it dawned on me that I was the smallest apprentice fitter and turner in the erecting shop. I was glad I had on my new hat, which I had worn with pride ever since I bought it. I had to be careful not to knock my head on the rods above me as I crawled under to where I had to put the split pins in the clevis pins. "No need to split the pins wide,

Number 5 steam crane

just enough so they won't come out," Alec said. I was getting on well with the job, when all of a sudden there was a loud explosion just beside the crane, with the unfortunate result that my head shot up and I hit it hard on one of the rods. "It's alright Gordy. It's alright Gordy. It's only the tyre furnace starting up," Alec assured me, and with that I finished the job and crawled back out. Alec said I had done a great job. This crane number 5, was one of two steam cranes (and number 7) built at the Newport Workshops in 1911. Each crane had an 80 psi (pounds per square inch) vertical steam boiler and twin 8 inch x 14 inch cylinder winding engines. They were rated at 30 tons at 18 feet and 14 tons at 30 feet.

Alec pointed down to some men working a little way over from the crane and said that it was the tyre ring burners being lit that I had heard. I had a look and lying flat on a big steel plate, was the centre of a wheel of a locomotive surrounded by a tyre that was being heated up by the ring of burners. After a while with a little smoke coming from the tyre as it was being heated, the tyre was lifted up by a small hoist. Using tongs, fitters carefully placed the hot tyre over the wheel centre. As they did they slipped thin steel sheets in between the wheel centre and its tyre. That was how I came to discover how flanged steel tyres were shrunk on to wheel centres.

While on the subject of cranes, one of the busiest workers at the Newport Workshops were the crane locomotives with their pip-squeak whistles, which were forever scurrying around the rail lines in the yard picking up bits of locomotives, wheels, castings and other items stored in the open along the rail sidings. All were within reach of the small crane's hook. Some of the rusty objects that lay beside the rails were in fact, part of the H class locomotives that were never built, due to post war rolling stock priorities. These 0-6-0 'Z' class locomotives

Number 3 crane locomotive
Photo VRCEPP

were some of the first locomotives built at the Newport Workshops. Why not 'A' class I thought, if they were the first to be built, I was not sure? They were originally used to haul some of the first suburban trains, later being converted to crane locomotives.

CHAPTER 10

THE CALL UP - A BIG DECISION AND THE WAR 1944

Spring was just about over and so was my time at the other college, the RMTC. Without telling my parents, I decided one evening after night school that I could no longer carry on, I just kept dozing off and that was no good at all. When I got home I told my parents and although they were disappointed, they realised that it was too much for me. They said don't worry, you are going to college at Newport, so it is not as though you are not advancing your education. I was not sorry that my hopes of getting an engineering certificate had come to an end, because I was fully engrossed in my apprenticeship in the railways and at that time that was all I wanted.

In the first week in May I received a letter from the Army notifying me that on the 19th May 1944 I turned 18 years of age, and was to be 'called up' or drafted into the army. Together with my father we looked at all the conditions and found that as an apprentice in a protected industry, namely the Victorian Railways I was exempt from the call up. My father said; "It's up to you son, you have the option, do you want to join the armed forces or stay where you are? I think the war is gradually nearing its end. If you take my advice you will stay where you are." My father knew quite a lot about the war. He read the papers assiduously and listened to the wireless, local radio and German radio on short wave. I think that despite the German propaganda the feeling he got from that source, was that the war for the Germans was not looking too good, especially considering their defeat on the Russian front, which he said was quite significant. So I decided to stay with the VR, which I must admit did not take a lot of persuasion. I could see too, the wonderful work that the Newport Workshops was doing to support the war effort, building Bren gun carriers, ocean going tugs, aeroplanes and of course the Garratts, so I had no feeling of letting our soldiers down by not joining the army. Talking with Kevin and Allan about this, Kevin had already had his call up papers and had opted to do the same as me and stay with the VR. Allan's birthday was not until later in the year, so he knew what to expect, and said that when the time came, he would probably make the same decision as us.

Less than a month later the news came through that on June 6th the long awaited decision to launch Operation Overlord was taken, where some 6,500 vessels landed over 130,000 allied forces on five Normandy beaches. That was great news and our thoughts were with them, hoping that the allied soldiers would succeed with not too many casualties. Even living in Rosanna I was seeing war training operations taking place, more like testing actually. On a large expanse of rising, open land on the eastern side of the Rosanna railway station, there was a dam filled with water. Bren gun carriers drove along Lower Heidelberg road and had great fun testing the carriers, tearing around the paddock and through the dam, throwing up great sheets of dirty, clay, coloured water. These carriers were being built in the gas works at Clifton Hill, another government instrumentality

A Bren gun carrier built at Newport
Photo VRBTRS

manufacturing equipment for the war effort. 1,844 Bren gun carriers were also built at the Newport Workshops.

Work on the Garratt was progressing well. The front water tank was brought over from the tender shop on a flat wagon and the crane lifted it on to the frame. We bolted it on to the frame and then shortly after the coal tender and its tank were delivered to us and this too, we bolted in place. Our new Garratt was not far from completion, most of the motion gear was in place on both units and we were just about to set the valve gear.

As usual on Monday afternoon I was off to College. Our class was still studying the construction and working of a modern steam locomotive and valve gears. The College had a demonstration board of Walschaert's valve gear. It showed all the components of the valve gear and how it worked. How the driver reversed the locomotive, how he could save steam by only admitting steam into a portion of the stroke of the piston letting the expanding steam do its work, referred to by the term 'cut off,' measured as a percentage of the full stroke.

Apprentices being shown the operation and components of Walschaert's valve gear
Photo VRBTRS

Having learned a lot about heat engines and locomotives in particular, we then learned about various systems related to railway rolling stock, the most important being the Westinghouse brake system. There was also another demonstration board and notes used to explain the operation and components of the safety, continuous brake system, fitted to virtually all rolling stock on the VR. Even though the weather was getting colder, as it was now winter, I still sat on the conduit ducting watching the trains go by, as I had during the summer and winter months.

A regular train that I saw at this time on most Monday mornings was a goods train that passed by about 12.15 p.m. just before it was time to go in to College. Most times it was hauled by a big 2-8-0 Consolidation C class, although sometimes it was an X class. As I have mentioned before, the Melbourne Road railway gates just by the Newport station must be the worst in Victoria for the short time they are open to road traffic. Sometimes the goods train had to wait just short of the crossing, down and around the long bend on the line by the workshops. Before watching this day, the C or X class had no trouble starting when the gates opened and the signal went off (down), but this day was different. The locomotive was a C class, which with clouds of steam and the noise of the locomotive losing its feet, as the driving wheels were not being able to get a grip on the rails although I was sure that sand would have been applied to the rails, the C class and its train did not move! Maybe it was a heavier goods train than usual, however, the signal went back to on (up) and the gates closed to the railway line.

The vehicles waiting to cross the line must have been very frustrated seeing no train go by. At last the gates opened again, only to close a short time later to let a train to Williamstown go by. While this was happening I saw the C class reverse a short way. Then it was time for the C to try again. The gates closed, the signal went to off and amidst a cloud of steam the locomotive, with its safety valve sending a jet of steam high into the air, at last got its footing and the C class with its long, string of wagons slowly came up and around the bend passing me just as it was time for College to begin. I was to see this performance repeated on quite a few occasions during that and the following winters. The railway line approaching these gates where any train, particularly a heavy goods train is held waiting for the signal to proceed, could not be worse from the point of view of starting a heavy train. It is on quite a steep grade and a curve, which is a combination of factors not conducive to starting a heavily loaded goods train, especially if the rails are wet.

The C class locomotive that had trouble starting on that and other days was a very powerful locomotive, the forerunner of the X class. It was not a handsome locomotive by any means, but the C class reminded me of ruckmen in the Victorian Football League of the time; the likes of Don McKenzie, Polly Farmer, Don Scott, John Nicholls and others who were not good looking, but possessed brute strength. They got the job done, which was how I described this C class locomotive. Compared to the earlier C class without smoke deflectors, I think the addition of these made them look much more powerful. The C class in particular was the one locomotive that I saw 'up close and personal,' working hard hauling its load regularly at lunchtime on a Monday before College and it became one of my favourite VR locomotives.

A C class 2-8-0 'Consolidation' locomotive
Photo VRCEPP

The half year exams were quite easy and I passed with good marks, but there was no exam requirement for the cube, it was an ongoing exam or test. As the weeks went by I cross cut chiselled the second side at right angles to the first side, then flat chiselled both sides. Finally both sides were chisel finished as flat as I could make them and the next operation was to use a flat second, cut file with the aid of the rule, to file the first side flat. I found that I really didn't like filing; it was hard work with nothing too much happening at once, certainly not like using the chisel, where bits of cast iron flew from the cube as the chisel bit in. Cast iron is a horrible metal to work with because it is full of dirty, black, graphite powder, which gets into the pores of the hands and it takes a lot to get them clean. However I kept at it as by now it was not a source of injury, but hard toil. Gradually the cube became an object of pride. Pride I think, with most of the class, because despite the hard work and some bruises we were all learning to use and master, some of the most important tools of our trade.

Back on the Garratt by the end of June we had completed G3 and it was ready to be put together, tested and driven. Because of College and the cube, I missed some of this, in particular seeing G3 under steam. Like G2. This disappointment was short lived, when I saw H 220 *'Heavy Harry'* being pushed into the erecting shop by a diminutive, crane locomotive. It was a great thrill to see this huge locomotive up close for the first time, especially when it was lifted up by the two 75 ton cranes and taken down to the far end of the shop and set on the rails. At lunch time I went and had a good look at her, (I mean him) and climbed into the cab, which was so much bigger than any other locomotive cab that I had ever been in. Evidently H 220 was not going to be in for long, only for an 'A' exam where the wheels, tyres, motion gear and ancillary equipment would be inspected.

A couple of days later, a fitter I did not know came and saw Vic and said I was to go with him as he had a job for me to do. Remembering the time when Alec Humphreys came and got me, I wondered if it would be another job for 'the smallest apprentice.' Time would tell. I walked off with this fitter; who introduced himself to me. His name was John and he took me down to the end of the erecting shop where H 220 was standing with some of its motion gear missing. John said to follow him up a ladder on to the top of the boiler. Just as well I didn't suffer from vertigo because it was quite high. We sat on top of the boiler where the steam and sand domes were located. The dome cover was off, which revealed some tubes (fire tubes) inside the boiler. "What I want you to do for me is to take this clevis pin, hop in there and crawl along the fire tubes a short way, where you will find the long regulator rod laying alongside an open connection to the regulator valve." "OK" I said, with the realisation that this was another job for 'the smallest apprentice.' John continued on; "Join the two together with this clevis pin and then come back and I will give you a split pin to put in and open it. Do you think you can do that for me?" "Yes I can." I replied.

It didn't look too hard as long as I didn't drop them. I only had to crawl along on the fire tubes the length of my body, so I got down flat and crawled along by the light of a lead lamp, found the rod and clevis and easily inserted the pin. I backed out, got the split pin and screw driver and put in the split pin and split it, which was really not too hard to do. Thankfully on this occasion there was no loud explosion to frighten me as I worked. I suppose it was not such a bad thing 'being the smallest apprentice' as it gave me a chance to be 'up close and personal' with H 220, and ever after when I saw H220, I was reminded of that day.

H 220 was one of three locomotives that were to be built at Newport Workshops to replace the use of double-headed, A^2s hauling *The Overland* to Adelaide, but after H 220 was completed in February 1941, the work on the other two was cancelled due to the advent of the war and construction for various reasons was not resumed after the war. The Allies had gained a foothold in France and were advancing, albeit with many causalities. Our war effort was going flat out with the aeroplanes, tugs, Bren gun carriers still being built and Vic and I were working on G4. Every now and again I got a chance to take a walk around the workshops. One of the surprising things I saw was in the turnery, over where the big wheel lathe was located. The lathe was operated by a young bloke with glasses.

Behind the lathe there was a collection of Communist posters, photos and slogans. Of course we were friends of the Russians at that time, because they were helping us to win the war. They had counter attacked and driven the Germans 300 miles west to Warsaw. This young bloke was a Communist and proud of it and was very happy with what his Russian comrades had done, even though I was sure he was an Australian. I talked to him for a while as I watched the big lathe tool take off large peelings of metal from the wheel as it was rotated in the lathe. I also had a look around the ocean going tug, which really fascinated me seeing this big ship being built by welders, electrically welding the hull plates and deck together.

Kevin Peterson had discovered that a little way up the yard there was a siding where locomotives were stabled before they were brought into the erecting shop. He said that some of them still had a few pounds of steam pressure left in them and suggested we go and have a look, so the three of us walked up the yard where we found an A^2. When we climbed into the cab we found it still had about 60 pounds of steam pressure showing on the gauge. We had a bit of fun playing with some of the controls, blowing the whistle, but it didn't sound too loud, then we turned on the turbo-generator, which made that lovely eerie sound. We opened the speed recorder and each of us took out part of the recorder graph for a souvenir.

One afternoon a week or so later on another locomotive, we took a step further. It was another A^2 as I remember, which this time had about 90 pounds of steam pressure left in the boiler. "Let's move it." Allan said. So we loosened off the handbrake and Allan put the valve gear in reverse. Allan knew a lot about A^2s because he had been working on them. He took hold of the regulator handle and opened it a little, then a little more until we heard a chuff, chuff, sound. The A^2 moved a short way in reverse and Allan very quickly closed the regulator. Because the siding was on a slope, the A^2 slowly rolled slowly back against the buffers. On the way back to the erecting shop, Allan suddenly exclaimed; "We forgot to open the release cocks, I hope we didn't do any damage!" The next time it happened we remembered to open up the release cocks, but it didn't matter because there was not enough steam to move the locomotive. The release cocks are valves operated by the driver, which are opened after a locomotive has been standing, even for short time, to expel any water condensate that has collected in the cylinders. If it is not removed, it could damage a cylinder. When locomotives are being photographed moving, the release cocks are usually asked to be left open by the photographer to make the photo look more impressive.

Back to the College and the cube, the last month of winter was upon us and the cube class were all more or less up to the filing stage. First one side then the other, getting it as flat and square to the other side as possible, which took some doing. I hated filing and all that carbon dust. However before long, I and most of the class had one side ready for scraping. Mr. Harman showed the class the items used for scraping. A faceplate, which has a very flat surface, Prussian blue, (a paste) and a scraper, a hand tool with a curved end, ground to produce two sharp edges. He showed us on a sample cube the mottled effect we had to achieve by the use of the paste on the faceplate, cautioning us not to use too much paste to get a reading. He showed us how to use the scraper and keep it sharp using a hand held, grind stone. Then we were off on our own. Scraping is a means of obtaining a very flat surface without the use of a machine and can be used on many other surface shapes and forms.

Having got the surface as flat as possible with a file, we used a faceplate a little larger than the flat side of the cube. With a finger, an even, thin, coating of Prussian blue is spread on the faceplate. The faceplate is then placed on the cube's flat surface and moved around a little before being returned to the bench. The face of the cube is then marked by the paste from the faceplate, showing the high spots on the surface. The scraper is used to scrape off these high spots by using the scraper first in one direction, then at right angles. This process is repeated over and over again until finally it is quite flat, shown by an evenly mottled, blue surface, produced by the application of less and less thinner coatings of paste on the faceplate as the surface of the cube becomes flat. I didn't mind scraping, it wasn't hard work and it was fascinating to see the surface of the cube gradually change from markings that were far apart, to getting closer and closer together as the surface became dead flat. It took about five mornings, or a just over a month to get the first side flat.

Mr. Harmon was respected by our class for his ability as an instructor. The knocks on the arm for strangling the hammer had been forgotten by most of us, or deemed efficacious to impart in the class the skill of using a hammer correctly.

CHAPTER 11

THE CUBE IS FINALLY COMPLETE 1944

It was now the time to work on the tasks that would complete this learning process, the fitting of two studs to one face of the cube and then use a shaping machine to cut two grooves at right angles on another side to fit a metal template. The class had to be split because there were not enough shaping machines for each member of the class. Some of the class went on the shaping machines, while the rest worked on making the studs, and I was one of them. Studs are used in many parts of steam locomotives, probably the most common being to fasten cylinder head covers to cylinders and the outer ring of a smokebox. Studs too are used in many industries as a means of fastening covers on all shapes and sizes of vessels, where a bolt and nut or tapped hole is not able to be used.

Studs on the driving and valve cylinders of a locomotive

Studs are threaded fasteners with a screw thread at both ends and a short unthreaded section in the middle. We first had to drill two tapping diameter holes to the correct depth in one side of the cube and then use thread taps, a taper, intermediate and plug tap, to cut a thread in the blind holes. When that was complete we were provided with a length of mild steel bar from which we cut two pieces with a hacksaw to the correct length for each stud. We were then shown how to use stocks and dies to form threads on each end of the studs, leaving one end very slightly oversize and on that thread, and make a shallow, hacksaw cut, diagonally down its length. Some of us wondered what the purpose of the hacksaw cut down the side of the stud was for. This was quickly explained to us by Mr Harmon. He said that because a cylinder head circumference may have as many as ten or more studs screwed into it, when the stud is inserted without the relieving hacksaw cut in the thread, the stud would trap a portion of air and compress it, with the risk that in time, cracks could form in the head.

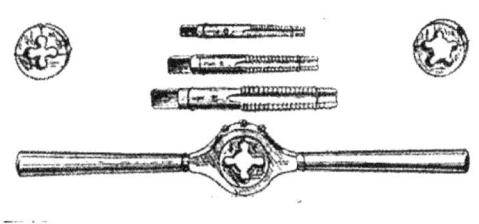

A set of taps and dies
Photo Ken Arnold

At last my turn came to use the shaper, which thrilled me no end. Using a centre punch, I marked out the shape of the slots I had to make to fit the template and placed my cube in the vice mounted on the shaper's table and tightened the vice securely. Mr. Harmon gave us a demonstration of how a shaper works, how the table with the vice can be adjusted both horizontally and vertically, either manually or using an automatic feeding mechanism. He showed us the electric motor that drives the reciprocating ram by a crank, and how the stroke of the ram can be adjusted. Finally the tool post and tool, which is attached to the ram clapper box and how the depth of the cut can be adjusted by the tool feed handle, so that as the ram moves forward it removes metal from the cube. Mr Harmon said that when we had the cube tightened securely in the vice, to come and get him and he would start up the shaper and guide us through its first strokes. I stood by the shaper examining all the controls until

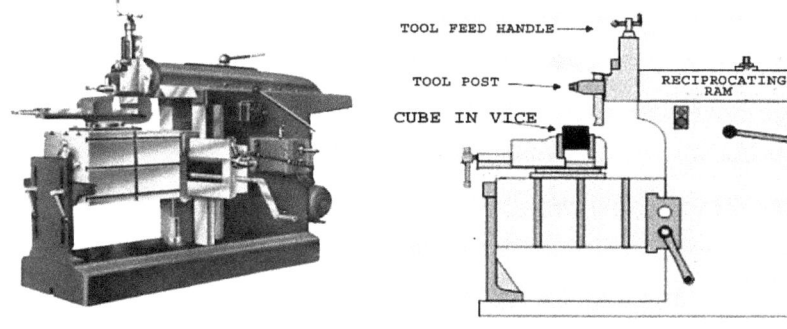

A shaping Machine

A diagram showing the front portion of a shaper and its main parts

eventually I saw that Mr Harmon was free and got him to come over to my shaper. He explained all the parts then opened up the side of the shaper to show me the crank that drove the ram. He adjusted the table and tool post to make the first cut. Then he started the motor and operated the start lever. I watched as the shaper went backwards and forwards, making the first cut in the cube. "Do you think you can go on from there now?" he asked me. "Yes." I replied a little hesitatingly. "Now if you have any doubts or problems, STOP the shaper and let me know, because you are now working with a machine that could cause you harm." This was his parting remark. A warning, which I of course I heeded.

I took a few cuts and slowly began to understand the adjustments I had to make, moving the table sideways and adjusting the depth of the cut, to achieve the correct size of the slot to fit the template, which I measured using another couple of new measuring tools, inside and outside callipers. Sometime later I had finished one groove and Mr Harmon checked it and gave his OK. I then turned the cube around and cut the other groove at right angles in the correct position to fit the template, which it did quite accurately. Mr Harmon gave his OK and that was just about the finish of the work on the cube. After operating the shaper doing that exercise I could really see how dangerous the shaper could be if its method of operation was not understood, or it was not used with caution.

When everyone in the class had completed the cube, which we more or less did at the same time, Mr. Harmon gave the class a short speech saying, how it had been a pleasure working with us. He impressed on us how important the skills we had learned in the class were to becoming fully competent in our trades. Finally he asked us; "What do you want to do with your cube, leave it here or keep it as a souvenir of your first year in the Victorian Railways as an apprentice?" I think, or I hoped we did, give him a clap and when I left I shook his hand and thanked him for his instruction and help. I elected to keep my cube and made a handle for it using the studs to attach the handle.

I took it home in the train and lugged it with many pauses to rest, up Hillside Road to my home where I proudly showed it to my parents. "What's that?" They at first exclaimed! Then I explained to them what it was all about, how it cost me many hours of hard toil to make it, the skills and the use of new tools I had learned in the process. "Good work," my father said. The cube was then used to hold open one of the doors in the house, but I can't remember exactly which one, nor do I remember what eventually became of it.

The cube class finished in the middle of December and I went back working with Vic on the Garratt. College too, finished about the same time. I did well in the exams as did my friends Kevin and Allan. In my last few weeks in the erecting shop I saw a few interesting sights, one very hilarious when I was watching a boiler being lifted off an N class in the next bay. As it was lifted clear of the wheels and frame, a head emerged from the firebox door. The boilermaker or fitter had obviously been sleeping in the firebox. He must have been a very sound sleeper not to have heard the lifting chains being attached. The other happening was when a *Spirit* locomotive, *Mathew Flinders* was brought in to the shop by a diminutive crane loco. When later the smoke box streamlined doors were opened wide on the hinges, an amazing sight met our eyes; the whole front of the smokebox right up the centre of the smokebox door was filled with grasshoppers, most of which cascaded down into the pit below. It must have run through a grasshopper plague somewhere between Spencer Street and Albury and they had been scooped up through the grill at the top of the doors. Of course poor, dribbling Harry got the job of disposing of them all. The *Spirit* didn't stay in for long, only a week while some adjustments were made to the valve gear. Maybe the adjustments were to the conjugating, valve gear, for the third centre cylinder.

.Just before I knocked off for Christmas, I got notification that beginning in January 1945; I was to attend College on Monday afternoon at 12.30 p.m. and Thursday at 8.00 a.m. Then a little later I was notified that when I returned from holidays, I was to report to Senior Foreman Ron Kennedy in the tender shop at 7. 30 a.m. I told Vic who said that I was probably going to work on the tug, which I should find very interesting. He said that I will probably return to the erecting shop sometime later in my apprenticeship.

During the first year of my apprenticeship I learnt a lot about my trade both at College and on the job. It was a most rewarding year in every way, especially working first hand on locomotives, meeting new people and making new friends. However, by far the most encompassing interest not directly related to locomotives and trains, but to learning new skills as a tradesman, was without doubt working on the cube. Although at times it was very difficult, especially the chiselling and probably the filing stage.

I had a very pleasant surprise when not only was I was issued with my new half fare rail voucher, but a free travel pass for use anywhere on the Victorian Railways. There were a few fitters who stayed on to work through the Christmas holidays, but Vic was not one of these. Christmas holidays began just before Christmas day. I said goodbye to Vic and thanked him for looking after me for the first year of my apprenticeship. I got together with Allan and Kevin and we wished each other a Happy Christmas. Both were remaining in the erecting shop to work next year, so we would be together at College on the same days, which was very pleasing. After the D Day landings, the Allies were making some advances on various fronts, but there was a big setback in a battle that killed many of our Allied soldiers during December in the Ardennes in France.

I saw a model locomotive I liked in one of the model shops and bought it for a good price. It was a tank locomotive with a 4-4-2 'Atlantic' wheel arrangement. I thought it looked a little bit like a D^4 4-6-2 tank locomotive used around the yards for shunting. They had shunter's running boards attached to them, so I decided to fit running boards to my new locomotive. I did not get it finished before the holidays came to an end, but I didn't mind because I would finish it later in the year. I would also get a single stage compressor made and attach that too. I had a great holiday with money to spend and when the time came, I was more than happy to return to the Newport Workshops to continue my apprenticeship.

Over the Christmas holidays with the Scouts we went on a few hikes, one around Warburton and it was great to be able to use my rail pass on that steam train journey to Warburton and return.

CHAPTER 12

YEAR 2 APPRENTICESHIP - THE TUG AND GARRATTS 1945

The day came when I went back to work to begin the second year of my apprenticeship and I settled back in the train in the plush, first class, compartment wondering what my second year experiences were going to be like, surely nothing to match working on the cube, although I learned a lot from that experience. It was a good feeling to alight on the Newport Workshops platform and wander over to the tender shop. The doors were closed, so I didn't see the tug until the doors opened and I went into the shop where it loomed up out of the semi darkness to reveal its welded hull, surrounded by scaffolding rising above me, an incongruous sight for the interior of a workshop where tenders for locomotives were constructed and maintained.

The 75 ft. ocean going tug under construction in the tender shop
Photo VRNLCN

I was eager to discover what sort of work I would be doing and I couldn't wait to find out. I found the foreman, who had an office at the back of the tug. I can't remember the foreman's name, but we shook hands and he introduced me to the fitter I was to work with, a bloke by the name of Jim Carter, a tall bloke with thinning, black hair, much older than Vic. Jim said I was to help him to drill holes in the tug's deck and hull. The whistle blew to begin work and we climbed up a ladder on to the steel deck of the tug. It was quite an awesome experience standing on the deck high above the workshop floor. The deck was open in the centre and I looked down to where I saw the large diameter propeller shaft, which disappeared through a bearing in the stern of the hull, but there was no engine installed at this stage. Jim explained to me that the hull was in its final stage of construction. He said the hulls were built in five sections and electrically welded and that we would be drilling holes in the bridge that was over in the carriage shops.

We left the tender shop and Jim took me over to one of the bays in the carriage shop where the large, steel, bridge structure was sitting on big wooden blocks. We climbed up a ladder on to the

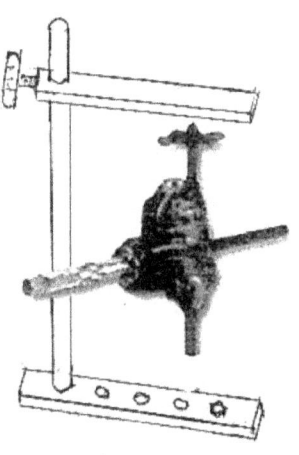

bridge floor, where the drilling machine was. Jim said we had to drill holes in the front, steel, wall of the bridge and we would be using the drilling machine, driven by compressed air through a long hose, which was used together with a drill stand (as shown in the accompanying diagram). The lower bar with the holes in it was for bolting the stand firmly to a drilled hole near to where the hole or holes had to be drilled. Jim said if a suitable hole was not available, a hole had to be drilled manually big enough to take a bolt to hold the base of the drill stand securely. The upper bar of the drill stand was adjustable for height and the loading screw on the top of the drill allowed force to be applied to the rotating drill of the machine. With a centre punch Jim marked the position of the hole we had to drill and we manhandled the heavy drill stand up to where we bolted it tightly to a hole already drilled in the plate.

Because we were drilling the hole in the vertical plate, getting the drilling machine and stand set up horizontally and bolting it in place was no easy task. We drilled a small pilot hole that was no problem, but then the drill had to be changed to drill the hole of the correct diameter, which if I remember was about 5/8" diameter. Every time we changed a drill in the drilling machine it had to be taken out of the stand and as I was to see this was a never ending task on this drilling job we were doing. The setting up of the drill stand however, wasn't the end of the difficulty of this job because the bridge plating was made of armour plated, steel, and when we began drilling, although Jim applied a copious quantity of brown cutting fluid to the drill bit to keep it cool, it very quickly became blunt and had to be sharpened continually because the armour plated steel was so hard. Sharpening the drill involved removing the drilling machine from the stand each time the drill was sharpened so altogether it wasn't an easy task for us.

Besides this the sound caused by the exhausting air from the drilling machine was quite loud and we were not using ear or eye protection that would have been mandatory at the time of writing. However, when Jim showed me how to sharpen the drill and grind the cutting edges to the correct angle and shape on the grinding wheel, we did this using goggles, and sharpening a drill was another new skill I learned drilling holes in the bridge.

Soon it was noon and I was off to College with the first morning of the second year of College in front of me. I met Kevin and Allan and we talked about our Christmas holidays and our new jobs. Kevin was now working with Vic on the Garratt, which pleased him no end and Allan was working on another A^2. The subject for this Monday afternoon was Mathematics. As soon as I sat down to begin the new subject, I realised it was a topic that I was quite familiar with, Algebra, so it looked as though I would have no trouble at College so far for the coming year.

The next couple of days I continued working on the tug with Jim who said that he had a labourer to help him while I was at the College. On Thursday morning I went to College at 8.00 a.m. for the second weekly class. The subject was an interesting one, Workshop Practice. This subject was of course a very important one for my trade. The first day the class was instructed in the use of various measuring instruments, micrometers, vernier callipers, dial gauges and the like. We learned by means of slides on a screen how to read the measurements of a micrometer, vernier callipers and height gauges. We practiced this on these measuring instruments, which were circulated around the class. This year was so different from last year, where our time in the workshop was interrupted by school and the cube, but now there were three days, Tuesday, Wednesday and Friday where I worked the full day, which gave me a much better continuity of work.

By the next couple of weeks we had finished drilling all the holes in the bridge and I had developed a few extra muscles because drilling the holes was quite hard work. We went to the tender shop taking the drilling machine and the stand with us, to drill holes in the deck of the tug for attaching brackets and other fixtures where the bridge would be fitted to the deck. These holes were much easier to drill, because the deck steel plating was not armour plate and the drilling was all able to be done with the drill and stand in a vertical position. There were a few pranks taking place around us on the welded deck, one concerning a wheelbarrow that was used to cart around various heavy, steel parts.

Sometimes, if a wheelbarrow was left standing for short time by its user, an arc welder would sneak up and tack weld the steel wheelbarrow wheel to the deck, which caused much annoyance when the handles of the wheelbarrow were picked up and an attempt was made to move it, however a few attempts would break the weld and that was it. Another similar trick was to weld the steel heel protector of a fitter's boot to the deck while he was standing and talking, but this required both the co-operation of the person he was talking to, not to let on and a very quick weld placed by the arc welder. On one occasion I saw the victim having to take his boot off and get a hammer and chisel to free the boot. All good harmless fun, which I don't think really held up our war effort to any extent.

At the end of January our family as usual went on holiday to Edithvale for two weeks, and I again had to get a ticket to take me from there to Newport Workshops. When I was arranging to get a ticket the same as last year, the ticket clerk told me that a train left from Aspendale direct to Newport Workshops, which he said would get me there before starting time. He told me the time it left Aspendale and sold me a concession ticket. It really wasn't that much further to walk to Aspendale than Edithvale to catch the train there, which meant I would not have to change trains at Flinders Street and that was a boon. The Newport Workshops train was parked on a siding overnight at Aspendale. The holidays were really great, but I never really got sunburnt, because going to work I was only was on the beach at weekends and after work.

Last year in the summer on the way to Newport, as the train began the climb up to Footscray station, I had noticed a strange smell. This year on a couple of hot mornings I smelt this again, only a lot stronger than I remembered from last year. It was a pungent, unpleasant, smell that I was told came from tanneries on the hill south of Footscray. Depending on the direction the wind blew and the temperature, it could sometimes really be quite objectionable. There was another sensory occurrence that I was aware of last year, but never took much notice of. This time it was not a smell, but a sound. Every now and again a loud roaring noise would split the air for a short time. It seemed to come from somewhere across the

The Newport power station

railway lines in the direction of Port Melbourne. I decided that Kevin might know what it was, so the next time I saw him, I asked him about the noise I had heard. "Oh; that's the safety valve blowing off at the Newport Power Station," he said. Every now and again at the time of writing, whenever I cross the *West Gate Bridge,* I get a glimpse of its tall chimney with the two red and white bands at the top of the chimney, as it stands tall above all around it, and I remember that at last, thanks to Kevin, I knew where the roaring noise came from. The Newport power station was built by the VR in 1918 as a coal fired power station to supply electricity to the suburban railway system, the Melbourne City Council Electric Supply Department, the Melbourne Electric Supply Company and the State Electricity Commission of Victoria (SEC). It generated 95.5 MW. In its life it underwent many changes and at the time of writing the power station is owned and operated by a private company.

The work I had been doing for the first half of the second year of my apprenticeship, was not of the type that I would have expected to be appropriate for an apprentice fitter and turner in the railways, that of serving my time working on a ship. Of course there was a war on and I was only too happy to do my bit towards the war effort. I must admit I found the experience interesting and instructive. I had been in fact been working on a locomotive during some of these months, but not a real one, on my make believe VR D4 class model locomotive that I bought during the Christmas holidays, but did not have time to finish adding the shunter's running boards and the air compressor. When I finally finished attaching the running boards it looked very good, quite like a D^4, except of course for its different wheel arrangement. It was really great to have a new locomotive to

The author's make believe model D^4   *A real D^4*

operate on my layout. I think it was made by Hornby, but I was not sure. It was not as good as my Lionel locomotive to operate, because to reverse it I had to move a little lever behind the cab. If I had known what I do now, I am sure that if I had made up a small switch to change the polarity of the rails that would have allowed me to reverse it and would not really have altered the control of the Lionel locomotive.

On the other hand the control of the Lionel locomotive to start, stop and move it in both directions was very easy. The control was by means of a form of what would be termed today, as a 'flip-flop.' Pressing the control button operated the following sequence: start-forward-stop-reverse-stop-forward, and so on. To make the locomotive stop and move forward again, two quick presses of the button would cancel the reverse motion and similarly forward could be cancelled. At that time I was not sure what type of mechanism made this happen. Both locomotives of course had good speed controls. The next addition to my layout was to construct a siding so that I could do some shunting and also use it as a place to store my rolling stock.

CHAPTER 13

VE DAY 1945 THE TUG AND AXLE BOXES 1945

In 1945 the war in Europe was showing some signs of success for the Allies. The Russians had liberated Auschwitz revealing the sickening, obscenity of the attempt by the SS to annihilate the Jews and the blitz of England was over except for the occasional V1 and V2 rockets dropping on London. The Western Allies lost the race to be the first into Berlin, beaten by the Russians who reached Berlin on 21st April. Hitler committed suicide on the 30th April and Germany surrendered on 7th May. At last the war in Europe was over. May 8th was celebrated as VE Day (Victory in Europe Day), and a holiday was declared in the British Empire. May 8th fell on a Tuesday, but the weekend after was declared a holiday in Australia to celebrate winning the war in Europe, even though the war against the Japanese in the Pacific continued.

Our Rover Scouts (the Warringal Rovers) quickly got together and four of us Ian Howard, Harry Gilham, Roy Quilliam and I decided to go on a bike ride over the three day Victory week end ride from Warburton across the ranges to Noojee. We travelled by steam train to Warburton and began riding from there along the Yarra River flats for about 8 miles, but after that most of the trip was a bike *walk*. We had to walk our bikes up the dirt road of the Reefton Spur and across the Great Dividing Range near Matlock. Some time ago, I had made pannier bags for my bike on my mother's sewing machine. The pannier bags hung from the carrier on both sides of the back wheel of my bike and carried most of the loose items I needed on the trip. In my rucksack, I only had my tent and sleeping bag and a few other oddments, which made it a lot easier to push and ride the bike. On the last night of our trip, we woke to find it had snowed during the night, but my hike tent did a great job keeping out the snow.

After a very uncomfortable breakfast in the snow, we mounted our bikes for the final leg of our ride to Noojee, which we knew was nearly 10 miles away all downhill, but first we had to push our bike pedals very hard to get through the snow covered road. Riding along a little further toward Noojee the road surface changed to the consistency of sticky mud. All of a sudden, we saw that Ian and his bike were in trouble. His plastic mudguards, had stuck to the wheels, which rotated as one with both mudguards torn from their supports, the front one finishing up in the front of his bike, like the antenna of a praying mantis. The rest of us had stronger steel mudguards, which also stuck to the wheels, but stayed in place, so we all had to walk our bikes through the sticky section. Luckily, a timber-jinker came along just then, and asked us if we wanted a lift to Noojee. Ian wisely accepted the ride, but the rest of us were looking forward to the downhill ride all the way down to Noojee, so we declined.

*On our bike ride
L to R the author Harry and Roy*

We were glad we did, because the sticky section was soon behind us and we had the joy of freewheeling the 10 miles, nearly all the way down to Noojee, where we met Ian. We decided to leave our bikes in Noojee and for a small charge, put them on the next train from there to Heidelberg and Rosanna, while we all caught a bus and train back to Melbourne. Our bikes arrived at our respective stations about three days later all in one piece, thanks to the efficiency of the VR. While we were away there had been great celebrations in the city, but soon it was all over and Australia then had to concentrate with the Allies, particularly the Americans, in winning the war in the Pacific.

I went back to Newport after the weekend, where nothing really had changed; it was work on the tug as usual. A week or so after we had drilled all the holes in the deck, we bolted the brackets on the deck ready for the bridge to be fitted. Jim said that we wouldn't be fitting the bridge to the deck, because after the propeller was fitted, the tug would be loaded on to a specially built, 32 wheel, low loader and taken to the Yarra where it would be launched and finally fitted up with the bridge, the engine and all the other fittings required to make it sea worthy. So that was the end for me of helping to build a ship.

Soon after working with Jim on a few odd jobs, I was informed that I was to be transferred to the 'axle shop.' I had visited this shop when Vic took me on a tour of the workshops and it was here that I saw the big, bronze, propeller for the tug being worked on, which was to be fitted to the tug. I said goodbye to Jim and thanked him for looking after me. He wished me well and I walked over to the axle shop and found the foreman Len Mitchell who I was to report to, a broad shouldered, fair headed, bloke. He said that I was to fit white metal bearings to wagon axles. My new job believe it or not, was scraping; not a cube, but white metal bearings, for railway wagon axle boxes. Every railway axle has two axle journals that revolve in white metal bearings, which support the weight of the vehicle. The most common type of bearings fitted to rail wagons, whether bogie or four wheel, is shown on the next page. The bearing components consist of the axle journal, the white metal bearing, a cotton oil pad and a small amount of oil, all of which are enclosed in

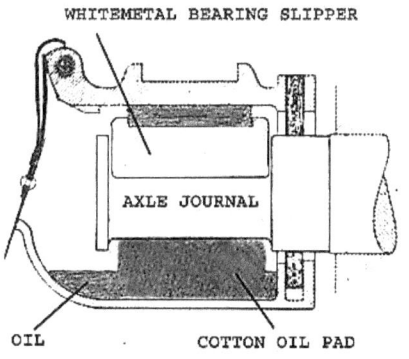

A diagram showing the axle box bearing components

A typical style of axle box

the axle box. The axle journal revolves in the white metal bearing that surrounds slightly less than half of the diameter of the journal, which is lubricated by a cotton oil pad sandwiched between the journal and the bottom of the axle box, and being partially immersed in the oil, it wicks the oil up so keeping the journal lubricated. The axle box has a strong spring loaded cover that keeps the dirt out and through which the oil can be topped up from time to time. The bearings require very little maintenance except to replace the oil and re-metal the white metal bearings.

Len showed me how to scrape the first bearing, putting a light coating of Prussian blue on the axle journal, then putting the bearing on the journal and rotating it around the journal a few degrees. He took it off, put it in the vice and proceeded to scrape away the high spots marked by the Prussian blue. The white metal was easy to remove with the scraper and it didn't take him more than about three or four markings, before he was able to show me the finish required of me, to fit the bearing to the journal. The same items were used to scrape the bearing as I had used to scrape the cube, Prussian blue paste, but the scraper was much different from the one I used on the cube. This scraper was like a very large, wood, spoke shave. It was about 16" long with a handle on each end and in the centre there is a shallow cupped blade, with two sharp cutting edges. I began on my first bearing, but it took me many more than four markings before Len was satisfied with my effort. However, like scraping the cube it got easier and in no time at all, I had become an accomplished bearing fitter. The bearing was quite heavy and had been re-metalled to conform roughly to the size of the journal, just having to be scraped to fit. During the first week I spent into the axle shop, I went a few times to have a look at the tug. It was still there, but when I had a look on the Monday after the weekend it was gone.

I discovered that in the Melbourne newspaper, *The Argus* on Tuesday 24th October 1944, there was a photograph of one of the tugs on the low loader with the caption: '*Built at Newport Railway Workshops for Munitions Stores and Transport, this 75 foot ocean-going tug had a clearance of only 1½ inches under Flinders street railway viaduct when it was taken to Victoria Dock entrance for launching in the Yarra. A special 32-wheel float was built to convey the tug to the dock.*' This explained why the bridge was not fitted to the hull, before it was taken away.

On the way home from work on 7th August 1945, huge headlines in the newspapers pronounced that an atom bomb, *Big Boy* had been dropped on the Japanese city of Hiroshima the previous day, with devastating and horrible consequences. Three days later, a similar headline announced that another atom bomb, *Fat Man* was dropped on a second Japanese city, Nagasaki. The result of the horrific devastation to the two, large, Japanese cities was that Japan surrendered on 14th August 1945. At last it was all over and we could relax.

I wondered what effect the end of the war would have on all the items that the Newport Workshops were making for the war effort, in particular the ones I had been working on, the Garratt and the tug. Back at work after that great news, most of the blokes were wondering like I was what changes this would bring to our working lives at the workshops. However life did not change in the axle shop and I continued on with my scraping.

CHAPTER 14

ATOM BOMB ENDS WAR – VR WAR EFFORT – THE ALPS 1945

It was only at the time of writing this book that I discovered what a huge and amazing role the Newport Workshops played in the manufacture of material and equipment for the war effort. Following is a record of these achievements published in the booklet *VICTORIAN RAILWAYS NEWS LETTER CENTENARY NUMBER SEPTEMBER 1954.* I have a 58 year old copy of this booklet, from which I have gained much information about the Victorian Railways during the war years when I was an apprentice. The cover of the booklet is shown on the left. Some of the war time products listed in the booklet are: *700 Beaufort bomber fuselages, 364 Beaufighter fuselages, 1,844 Bren gun carriers, 1,000,000 aircraft ammunition shells of various sizes, 40,000 forgings of 26 different types of instruments, an order for 8 ocean going tugs and steam engines, 12,000 electrical meters, 482 complete sets of generating and battery charging equipment,*

moving targets for army tank crews, 60,000 tarpaulin products of various shapes, sizes and types, repairs to equipment belonging to the R.A.N, U.S. Navy, Royal Netherlands Navy and the Merchant Service, 98 E class 40 ton gondola trucks, 2 60 ton wrecking cranes, an ambulance train and of course last, but not least from my point of view 12 Garratts. With regard to the tugs, I am not sure how many were built, I suspect only two.

It makes me very proud to have served in the VR in those years, although I was quite unaware at the time that all this was going on in the huge complex of the Newport Railway Workshops. I am also not sure, how soon the production of all the above items for the war effort was wound down, but I believe that the changeover was quite rapid. I was aware that the next priority for the workshops was to carry out a lot of maintenance to the railway infrastructure and rolling stock that had deteriorated during the war years. There was however, an interruption to this resumption of railway work, when on Tuesday 28th August a 24 hour railway strike was called over shift work by some railway unions, and as a consequence all suburban trains were cancelled, so I had a holiday because I could not get to work, but my father managed to get to work in the city on a couple of connecting buses.

Life after the war at home, carried on much the same as before the war, although we were all five years older and I suppose more 'worldly' than before. We wondered what the heck we would do with the air raid shelter that we dug, but thankfully we did not have to use. My father as usual came up with a great idea, we would not fill it in, but we would use it to store our large, yearly, harvest of apricots. Wonderful news came through to our next door neighbours Mr. and Mrs. Downs. Their son Jack was alive and well. After his aircraft was shot down in an air raid, he was rescued and hidden in an attic by a Dutch family. It would be a great and thankful homecoming and we looked forward to seeing him soon. Most of our street knew Jack, and were very concerned when he went missing and delighted with the news that he was alive.

I continued on with scraping bearings and found out that my foreman Jim Mitchell, a great bloke, was the Commodore of a sailing club, I think it was Williamstown, he looked the part too, with his fair hair, broad, shoulders and strong body. I could just imagine him all dressed up in his Commodore yacht garb. Scraping bearings was not a hard job, but it did become a little boring so ironically, I looked forward to my half days at College. I met Kevin and Allan at school and Kevin said he worked on the last Garratt to completion and then went back working on other locomotives. Towards the end of the year a notice came to our Rover crew from Rover Scout Headquarters, informing us that a party of Rovers Scouts was required to carry out maintenance work on the Rover Scout Chalet on the Bogong High Plains (BHP). I had heard about this chalet, where parties of Rover Scouts went to spend a fortnight skiing in the Alps of North East Victoria. I decided I wanted to be included as a member of the work party, which would give me a wonderful opportunity to see the high mountains of Victoria.

I was the only member of our crew who was free to go on this work party for a week, so I applied to be one of the parties. Very soon after I received a letter from the Brighton Rover crew telling me they were going by car and to meet them at 8 a.m. on Boxing Day morning on the corner of Bell Street and Sydney Road Cobourg. My second year at College came to an end and I did well in the exams. I was given my rail pass and half fare ticket voucher before I knocked off for Christmas and with a Merry Christmas wish to Kevin and Allan and other work mates, I was off for my Christmas holidays.

I was home for Christmas this year and was looking forward to my journey to the Alps. After a succulent Christmas dinner and day with my family on the following morning Boxing Day, I said goodbye to my family and with my rucksack on my back filled with my sleeping bag and other essentials, I took a bus to the corner of Sydney Road and Bell Street. I couldn't believe my eyes when around 8 a.m., two old cars pulled up with their Rover Scout passengers. I was to travel with Skipper Dudley and his son Len and three other Brighton Rovers in their car, a canvas top Chevrolet. The other car was a large Vauxhall, both 1927 models, the year of my birth! After being introduced to all the Rovers, both cars started off together along the Hume Highway, travelling along at quite a good pace. Riding along in the Chevrolet with the sides open to the wind and the high canvas roof above was great fun, especially as I had never been beyond the Great Dividing Range to the north of Melbourne before.

At Wangaratta we turned on to the road along the Ovens valley, passing through the town of Myrtleford, and then on towards Bright. As we passed Mt Buffalo to the west, I gazed in amazement at its rocky walls and lofty heights, never having seen such a spectacular mountain range like that before except in photos. After passing through the beautiful township of Bright we turned on to a dirt road that led up to the Tawonga Gap, high above the valley floor. Both cars were stopped to check the water in the radiators, then off we went driving up the rough dirt road, which wound its way around many sharp curves as it climbed steeply towards the summit of the Gap. Both cars climbed without overheating, which was remarkable for such old cars as it was quite a hot day. We eventually reached the summit of the Tawonga Gap, a saddle at a height of 2,898 ft. that separates the Ovens Valley from the Kiewa Valley.

What a great revelation it was when we got out of the cars! The view was breathtaking; I had never seen anything like it before, even surpassing the rugged cliffs and gorges of Mt Buffalo that I had just seen. Skipper Dudley pointed out various features of this glorious panorama. The horizon was dominated by the huge bulk of Mt Bogong, 6,508 ft. (1.984 m) the highest mountain in Victoria.

Below us lay the valley of the Kiewa River, with the tributary valley of Mountain Creek leading up to the horizon, from which the long, steep, Staircase Spur led up to Mt Bogong's summit. This was the first time that most of the Brighton Rovers had, like me, seen this glorious panorama and a couple of them vowed that they must climb Mt Bogong sometime. I certainly felt that I must too.

We climbed back into the cars and descended the steep, rough, winding road on the other side of the Gap to Mt Beauty. The descent was made to the sound of a gentle hissing from the engine of the wonderful old Chevrolet, brought about by the turn of a knob on the dashboard. This activated a form of air brake that was called 'engine compression braking.' It was very effective, although I never found out quite how it worked, but it got us safely down to the floor of the beautiful Kiewa Valley, where we passed through a gatehouse to the State Electricity Commission's (SEC) town of Mt Beauty that was being built to house families working on the Kiewa Hydro-Electric Scheme, under construction in these mountains.

Leaving Mt Beauty the water in the radiators was checked again, ready for the next big climb of nearly 5,000 ft. to the Rover Scout Chalet. After passing through another gatehouse, the cars commenced the climb up the winding, rough, gravel road. We had great views of the high mountains

The Vauxhall and The Chevrolet stop for a rest on the way up the Upper Kiewa Valley Road near Bogong

above and around us as we passed by the village of Bogong and some camps along the way. We also saw earth works being carried out on a dam. All the way as the car climbed up the road there were forested mountains surrounding us, the names of which none of us knew. After crossing a bridge over a swiftly flowing river, the road climbed higher and higher and the tall trees began to thin out, until a few miles further on, they just about disappeared completely at a place I was told was called Falls Creek. From then on the rough road came to an end and we drove across an undulating plain into a world of stunted gum trees, with the ground covered by short, tufted, grass and beautiful wildflowers. We appeared to be on the top of Victoria.

The final part of this wonderful drive from Melbourne was along a ridge on a two-wheel dirt track, the only land rising above us being a few mountain peaks. We parked the cars on the top of this ridge, which I found out was called the Rocky Knobs. The cars never caused us any trouble at all; they both did wonderfully climbing up the mountains without boiling. We walked down a small valley amid wildflowers and bushes to a large, galvanized, iron clad building, the Rover Scout Chalet where we were welcomed by the Rover Scout Commissioner Bill Waters and other rovers already in residence.

The Rover Scout Chalet

The Chalet built into a slope above a small stream called Middle Creek consisted of two levels. The ground floor was the living area, containing a stove and cooking area, a large fireplace and eating section, with large rough timber tables and benches. A wash room, toilet, shower and wood storage room was located adjacent to the main living area. After a large meal and a sing song we all retired to the sleeping quarters accessed by means of a vertical wooden ladder to an upper level where everyone laid out their sleeping bags on straw paillasses on the large flat floor for a good night's sleep.

The next morning after a filling breakfast of porridge, bacon and eggs, we were assigned various jobs to do around the Chalet for the next few days, cutting and collecting wood, painting and repairing various items of equipment. During the week some rovers got together to ask Bill Waters if we could go on a hike to Mt Bogong. He said that if we finished everything that needed to be done, he would lead a party to Mt Bogong with those who wished to go, on the last two days of our stay December 28th and 29th, so we worked very hard and got all the jobs completed.

Early on the morning of the 28th, ten of us left the Chalet carrying food and camping gear, which had been divided up equally amongst us. One rover had only a big, billy can full of eggs suitably packed so they wouldn't break. This was very awkward to carry, so we all took turns at egg carrying. We set out north across the Bogong High Plains (BHP), walking along an undulating track through the snow grass and wildflowers that covered the ground. We passed a herd of cattle that turned their heads around to look inquisitively at us as we walked by as we skirted around the western side of Mt Nelse 6,175 ft. (1.882 m).

Directly ahead of us the long, high summit ridge of Mt Bogong with a couple of snowdrifts still showing in its steep gullies confronted us on the northern skyline. After passing by Roper's Hut, a cattleman's refuge, we descended down a ridge called Duane's Spur, which dropped down steeply into the deep valley of the fast flowing Big River, which separates the BHP from Mt Bogong, We forded the river without any trouble, before ascending a ridge called the T Spur. This was a very, steep and exhausting climb of around 3,000 ft. through tall timbers.

Finally we rose above the trees on to a ridge and a grassed meadow, where we found a very substantial, stone walled hut, called The Cleve Cole Memorial Hut, on Camp Valley, which was to be our campsite for the night. After we had eaten a tasty stew and had a cup of tea, Bill Waters told us about the tragedy that befell Cleve Cole and two other men, all friends of his, and how he was a member of the rescue party. Tired after a long day, I slept soundly on the soft snow grass beneath my groundsheet.

The Cleve Cole Memorial Hut

We woke early next morning to another fine day and after breakfast we got away walking up the long, south-east ridge to Mt Bogong's summit, admiring as we went the view back to the BHP. Soon we reached the large, rock cairn, on the summit of Mt Bogong (6,508 ft.), where we each took a turn to climb up to the top of the cairn, to be the highest person in Victoria. The view in all directions from the summit was immense. To the north the mountains bordering the Kiewa valley, to the west Mt Buffalo, while to the south Mt Feathertop and Mt Hotham stood out above all the others. Away on the eastern skyline, the Great Dividing Range of NSW contained the only mountains we could see that we knew were higher than us, the highest of these being Mt Kosciusko 7,328 ft., 820 ft. (250 m) higher than Mt Bogong.

Before we left the rover chalet I asked Bill Waters, who knew me very well, if it would be possible for me to be invested as a rover scout on the summit of Mt Bogong. I told him I had completed all the necessary preparation requirements. He said he would be pleased to carry out the investment ceremony, provided we had time and the weather remained favourable. After we all had a good look from the summit, Bill Waters brought us together, just below the cairn on the north side overlooking the Kiewa Valley and the Staircase Spur.

With that wonderful view in front of me, I was invested as a Rover Scout in a simple ceremony that was basically a reaffirmation of the

Scout Laws. Bill Waters conducted the investiture ceremony, with all the other rover scouts as witnesses to the promises I made.

After everybody had shaken my hand, we began hiking to the west along Bogong's summit ridge towards the West Peak 6,435 ft. This peak is not usually considered as being the second highest mountain in the state, but as part of the Bogong massif. The panorama from there was as awe inspiring as that from the main summit. We were looking straight down on to Little Bogong, Mt Beauty and Tawonga, while in the far distance the Ovens Valley along which we had driven only a week ago, was clearly visible

Leaving the West Peak we continued on our way down the steep and rocky, Quarts Knob Spur. This brought us to a low saddle from which we had a steep climb back on to the BHP. It was now late afternoon as we made our way back towards the Rover Scout Chalet past Basalt Hill, where darkness quickly descended. We had a few torches, but soon the batteries ran out so we continued along in single file with the Rover Scout in front, telling the Rover Scout behind him what to look out for, a rock, dip, bush and so on. In this way under Bill Water's guidance we arrived back at the Chalet around midnight. So concluded our impromptu, very fast, but very enjoyable hike over the BHP to Victoria's highest mountain, a wonderful experience that brought to a close our Rover Scout work party. After a cup of tea we went upstairs to our sleeping bags, and as can be imagined, I went quickly to sleep.

We rose early the next morning and got ready for our long journey back to Melbourne. We thanked Bill Waters for taking us on the wonderful hike, and then after shaking hands with all the others we set off back up to where the cars were parked on the Rocky Knobs. The cars were quickly started up and we were on our way down the Upper Kiewa Valley Road past the village of Bogong and as we drove along, I got a glimpse of the Quarts Knob Spur down which we had descended yesterday. On through Mt Beauty we drove and up the steep climb to the Tawonga Gap, where we stopped for a short while to admire the magnificent view of Mt Bogong. This time however, with the realisation and thrill that I had actually trodden on that lofty summit. Leaving Tawonga Gap, we drove back down the winding, rough road, to Bright, where we had lunch. Then on along the Ovens valley past Mt buffalo, which brought to mind a very unique event that I remembered seeing in the papers and on the newsreels in my youth.

Mr. Parkinson a licensee of a hotel in Beechworh bet Mr. Evans a Beechworth garage operator £20 that he could not wheel him in a wheelbarrow to the Mt Buffalo Chalet in eight days, a distance of just over 50 miles. In June 1935 Mr. Evans won the bet pushing Mr. Parkinson up the mountain with the last few miles through a snow covered road!

Somewhere near where the Hume Highway ran close by the railway line near Wallan just over The Divide, Skipper Dudley brought our cars to a halt and suggested we walk across to a small embankment by the railway line. He must have been aware that the *Sprit of Progress* was due to pass by because very soon we heard the thrilling sound of a locomotive chime whistle. It was beginning to get dark and in no time at all a locomotive and train came speeding toward us, its bright, headlight lighting up the rails brilliantly ahead of it. When I got my first glimpse of the front of the locomotive, I saw it really was *The Spiritof Progress*, which sped by with the fascinating spectacle of seeing all the polished steel, motion gear, whirling around, lit up by lights concealed under the streamline panels.

It was a thrilling experience watching the passenger carriages and the observation car with their windows lit up in yellow lights disappearing quickly into the fast fading light. I told Skipper Dudley that I was an apprentice at the Newport Workshops, saying I was not aware that *The Spirit's* motion gear was illuminated at night. We finally arrived at Coburg after sunset, where I left the others after thanking them all for the great journey, especially Skipper Dudley and his wonderfully, reliable, old Chevrolet. After a handshake all round, I boarded a bus to take me home to Heidelberg. Thus came to an end my fabulous journey to the Victorian Alps, and seeing *The Spirit* in such an awesome manner, a picture I can still see in my mind's eye to this day.

I still had a week left before my holidays were over, so I decided to have a look at my Lionel locomotive that sometimes did not obey the start, stop, sequence as it should. With my father's help we pulled it apart, which revealed the way the control sequence operated. We found that the core of a solenoid was attached to a short arm that in turn operated a ratchet, which on each press of the button, rotated a small, plastic drum on which were moulded, copper segments. These in turn came in contact with thin, copper, contactors that switched circuits to control the locomotive with the start, stop, forward, reverse sequence. The trouble was that these contactors were worn out at their ends and were not making good contact with the copper segments. What to do? We got some copper strip, cut it to size and soldered it to the existing worn contactors, put the locomotive together and it worked perfectly again. Not only that, but I had learned a bit about the action of DC solenoids. By that time my Christmas holidays were over I was looking forward to going back to begin the third year of my apprenticeship.

CHAPTER 15

YEAR 3 APPRENTICESHIP – BRAKES, EASTER AND SKIS 1946

After the Christmas holidays it was good to get back on the 6.10 a.m. train again and travel to the Newport Workshops. I went back to my job of scraping bearings and very soon I received notification that College was about to begin again for two half days as usual, but which days and times they were I cannot remember, The subjects were Engineering Drawing and the other one was Physics.

My family's holiday was again at Edithvale and this year as usual our holiday was in a house on Pt. Nepean Road. There was a vast difference from the former years as it was now the first year after the war and the traffic on the roads had grown considerably. I had not seen any troop trains, but instead saw a few D^3s hauling regular, scheduled, passenger trains to destinations beyond Frankston on the Mornington Peninsula. Red Hill, Mornington and Stony Point.

With regard to the number of motor cars to be seen, petrol rationing had been relaxed and people lucky enough to have cars were enjoying the summer, going on drives that they could not do during the war years. We were always at Edithvale on the Australia Day holiday weekend January 26th and this year the traffic on Pt. Nepean Road was very heavy all day. Just on dusk everybody, it seems, after having had a wonderful summer's day on the beach or elsewhere on the Peninsula must have decided it was about time for them all to head back home towards Melbourne. The result was that there was a traffic jam with mile upon mile of cars slowly moving about walking pace along the road. Some cars pulled out on to the side of the road from time to time for a rest, or because their radiators were getting too hot. It was not until after sunset, before the jam eased and the traffic thinned out. Not since then have I ever seen such traffic on that road, now called The Nepean Highway.

It was good too to be back at College with my good friends Kevin and Allan again and hear how they had been shifted around the workshops on various jobs. Kevin was working in the tender shop, working on tenders not on a tug because the tug I worked on was the last one built at the workshops. Allan was working in the turnery on various machines mostly lathes. At College I enjoyed both subjects Engineering Drawing and Physics, especially Engineering Drawing, where we had drawing boards to work on and were supplied with all our drawing needs. After College I got together with Kevin and Allan, and told them how I had seen the *Spirit of Progress* speeding along on the way to Albury in the dusk, and how its motion gear was lit up beautifully by lights under the panels. We determined that next time a *Spirit* was in the shop we would go and have a look for the lights.

I worked for about two months in the axle shop before I was transferred to the brake shop to work cleaning up bronze, castings before they were nickel plated, but I never saw where this was done. Cleaning up involved removing casting burrs with a file and once again it was not a hard job just a boring one, at which I learned nothing new. While I was there I watched from a distance, but with great interest the latest intake of apprentices toiling away at their cubes. I also had a good look at the foundry, the huge furnaces, the sand moulds for the castings, the steaming hot, completed castings of all shapes and sizes. I rather liked the pleasant smell that pervaded the foundry, which I thought came from the sand and the hot steel. There was another smell and sound that was new to my nose and ears that I found came from vats, which contained a simmering, mixture of some grey liquid in which various large and small items were suspended. The noise coming from the vats sounded like gravel being stirred around in a cement mixer and the smell was something like cabbage. I was told that these vats were cleaning baths where oily, dirty parts were cleaned prior to being repaired and the gravel noise I heard was the steam slowly bubbling through the cleaning fluid.

I only worked on cleaning up castings for a short spell before I was transferred to another part of the brake shop, this time to work on the equipment that gave the shop its name. Brakes! The foreman I reported to sent me over to a fitter and we introduced ourselves to each other, but I can't remember his name, so I will call him Fred. He said I was to help him work on triple valves. He explained that a triple valve was part of the Westinghouse, compressed air, braking system fitted to most railway rolling stock, wagons and carriages. Fred showed me a triple valve in pieces and then took me to a bench with a vice and showed me a dirty triple valve. He said: "First of all give it a good clean with the wire brush and then I will show you how to take it apart and what to do next.

I began cleaning the valve, which was not an easy job, but I finally got all the dirt off down to the brass body. I showed it to Fred who was happy that it was clean enough and using various special tools I watched him as he took the valve apart and put the parts side by side on the bench. Inside I found a rubber diaphragm and some other parts. Fred showed me how to clean the inside with some fluid, and then he examined it all and said the valve would need a new diaphragm and a couple of other parts that were worn. He got these and showed me how to put it back together using a little light oil.

"Now we have to test it, but before that I will show you how the Westinghouse brake system works." He drew a diagram for me on a piece of paper outlining the main components fitted below each

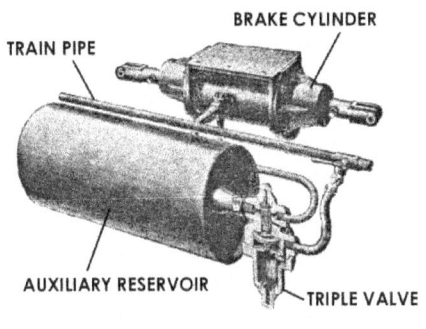

Shown above are the main components of the Westinghouse brake system as fitted to all rolling stock.

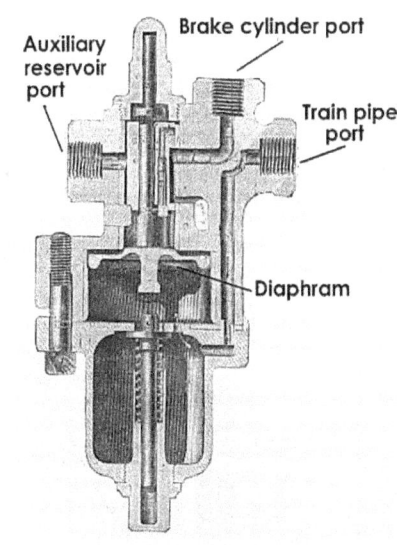

TRIPLE VALVE CROSS SECTION

wagon or carriage. Fred drew various lines connecting the triple valve to an auxiliary reservoir, a brake cylinder and labelled one of the pipes the 'train pipe,' which was connected continuously with every train pipe on each wagon and eventually to the driver's brake valve in the locomotive.

Fred then set up the triple valve in the test rig connecting the ports to gauges on the test board and moved handles that applied air at range of pressures to the valve and by watching the pressures shown on gauges declared that the triple valve was working OK. "Can you take apart the next one?" "Yes." I said. "Show me when you have got it all apart." That took up nearly a whole day and from then on except for the interruptions of going to College I worked on triple valves, but always after having taken them apart. It was Fred who decided whether a new diaphragm or other parts needed replacing. After I had put the valve together, I helped Fred test them. After working on triple valves I worked on locomotive driver's brake valves, cleaning, dismantling, replacing worn parts, reassembling and testing, always under Fred's supervision. I also helped in the heavy work of maintaining and repairing brake cylinders and air reservoirs, however I do not remember seeing or working on engine air compressors, those units attached to a locomotive that make that enchanting panting noise, keeping pressure in the train line and the auxiliary cylinders, when the locomotive is at rest. I never did find out where the air compressors were made and maintained and never thought at the time to ask.

Triple valves are so called because they perform three functions: (1) Direct air from the train pipe to charge the auxiliary reservoir. (2) Redirect air from the auxiliary reservoir to the brake cylinder proportional to that in the train pipe. (3) Apply and release the brakes. Put simply, the triple valve is a form of pressure regulating valve, which is under the control of the driver of the train. The other important components; the driver's brake valves, brake cylinders, main and auxiliary air reservoirs and air compressors, make up a complete system. I had learned about the Westinghouse brake at College and had read about it in my railway books, but I didn't tell Fred this, because if I did I thought he might not tell me any more about it and I am sure there was a lot more to know, and of course there was.

The vacuum brake has been used for continuous braking on most English passenger trains, but is limited in the force that could be applied to brakes because the amount of air pressure was a maximum of just less than 15 psi of vacuum or 'negative pressure' available to be converted to a braking force, whereas in the Westinghouse brake system the pressure available is in the order of 100 psi of 'positive pressure.' Furthermore many English goods trains had no continuous braking, relying on the locomotive's brakes and the brake van at the end of the train. Most of the four wheel

English railway wagons in those years were coupled by simple three link couplings, which it was said quite correctly that it made starting a heavy goods train easy, because the slack between each wagon and its load was taken up gradually. While on the subject of English railways, this brings to mind too, the fact that English steam locomotives did not have powerful headlights, only small marker and destination lamps, nor did they have cow catchers only wheel guards. The reason given for these differences that I had read about in English railway books was that all railway lines in the UK were fenced and that headlights would diminish a driver's night vision- believe it or not.

Easter came around and together with four of our Rover Scouts I went on a hike for a couple of days into the tall mountain ash forests beyond Warburton. Our hike took us a few miles out of Warburton and up into the ranges along bush tracks where the forests were just beginning to recover from the 1939 fires and new green growth was sprouting from the huge, bare trunks, of what was left of the original, tall mountain ash trees. We came to one of the main timber mills, the Federal mill and it was at this mill that some of this burnt timber was being logged and cut to size with large revolving saws, while behind the mill there was a huge pile of orange and brown sawdust, evidence of the amount of log cutting that was still taking place at the mill.

The Federal timber mill

After being cut to size the logs were transported on a different form of railway system than any of us had ever seen before, or even thought was possible. From this mill came a 'timber tramway,' a rough railway line that wound its torturous way down through the forest towards the large timber mills from where the logs were being cut at various locations in the forests.

We followed one of the tramways for a long way, the rails of which for long straight stretches, were made of planks of hardwood, but on the many sharp curves and over trestle bridges iron rails were used. The method of transporting the large freshly, sawn logs on the tramway was to chain securely one end of the log to a short, steel, four wheel bogie truck and the other end to another for wheel bogie, making a bogie railway truck the length of the log. These 'bush bogies' as they were called, were constructed of wood and were connected with pipe bars about 6 feet long. The bogie wheels were about 15" diameter with rims some 6" wide and 2½" flanges, to insure that when running along the wooden rails they had very little chance of derailing. There were also various forms of manually operated, hardwood, block brakes used. The bogie trucks carrying the logs and sawn timber were coupled in twos and threes along the tramways by various means, draught horses, small steam locomotives and diesel tractors.

The tramway with timber rails

We spent the night alongside a bush track just out of Powelltown and the next morning we followed the Powelltown railway line, a few miles east of Powelltown, or what was left of it as it had been closed sometime earlier. Here the line went through a 1,040 ft. (317 m) long tunnel, which we walked through, a rather spooky and dank experience. The tunnel was later boarded up. Hiking on for some miles after passing through the tunnel, the former

One of our scouts ascending the High Lead

tramway turned to go straight up the mountainside. This was called the 'High Lead', where logs were lowered on rails by cable from the Federal and Ada mills that were close by. Following various tram tracks we finally left them and walked back down the mountain on bush tracks to the same camp site where we had camped the previous night.

The next morning Easter Monday, the last day of our hike, we went through Powelltown and had a look at the large timber mill there, which was served by a three foot (910 mm) gauge railway line with steel rails that ran from beyond Powelltown to Yarra Junction.

Leaving the mill where I saw one of the diesel tractors used on the railway line and after having a good look there, we left and followed the well-constructed narrow gauge railway line that carried the timber from the mill to Yarra Junction where the sawn timber was transferred to VR wagons.

A Diesel tractor at Powelltown

Instead of waiting a long time for the train we caught a bus in Yarra Junction, which took us back home after a very interesting and informative hike amongst some of Victoria's timber country, where I saw a railway system of much different construction and method of operation than the VR. Sadly the tramlines we saw and hiked along no longer exist, so present day hikers in these mountain ranges can no longer admire the ingenuity of the timber getters, nor use these tramlines for easy access around the forests. I was fascinated to see railway lines made of wooden planks and how effective and simple they were as an alternate form of railway line used in timber getting. An excellent book *Powelltown* by Stamford, Stuckey and Maynard documents the history of the timber mills and tramways in the forests surrounding Powelltown.

Since going on the work party to the BHP with the Rover Scouts last year, staying in the Rover Scout Chalet and hearing and seeing photos of skiing around the BHP, my interest in the sport was growing. I hoped that next year I might be able to go skiing with the Rover Scouts and that was to be my other challenge, besides becoming a tradesman.

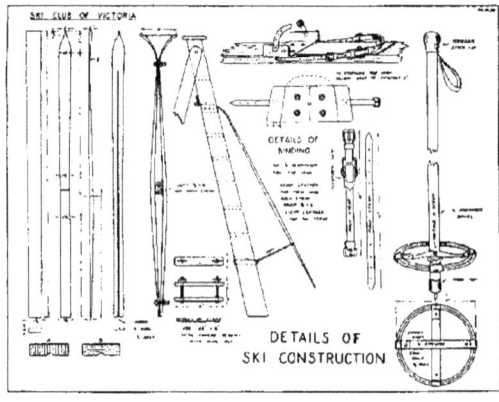

The instructions for making skis

I had completed making a siding for my model railway and now all my spare time was devoted to the next big job that of making a pair of skis in readiness for going skiing with the Rover Scouts on Mt Donna Buang next winter. Ready-made skis were very expensive, but our Rover Scout crew had been supplied with instructions printed in the Victorian Ski Club's March 1936 magazine *Schuss* on how to make skis very cheaply, so most of our Rover Scouts decided to make their own. This involved purchasing a pair of ski blanks from the Tasmanian Timber Bending Company that already had the turn up and camber steamed into them. Back at the Preston Technical School I had a distinct dislike for working with wood, but I had to overcome this and virtually learn a new trade. The work required cutting the blanks to shape, making the central groove and fitting the steel edges and bindings. I commenced shaping the blanks with chisels, planes, rasps and other wood tools, fashioning the ski blanks to the desired classic shape by following the drawings and instructions supplied. I purchased the steel edges and bindings from Andy Broad, whose shop was the only shop in Melbourne at the time that sold ski and camping gear. I made my own ski stocks from bamboo and leather strapping and converted my walking boots to make them suitable for ski boots, by cutting a groove in each heel and screwing angle pieces of steel into the insteps to prevent the boots from buckling in the ski bindings.

In the process of making the skis however, I sliced off a large flap of skin from my thumb. This calamity happened on a weekend, but it did not bleed much and I had to be *'rushed'* to the doctor at Ivanhoe. With a heavily bandaged thumb my father took me down to the railway station, where we had to wait for about forty five minutes for a train, because we had just missed one. At last the train came and we were off to see the doctor. The doctor attended to me straight away, but he never stitched it up, just bandaged it tightly. It healed OK, but I still have the scar today. The bindings for the skis in which the ski boot is secured to the ski, consisted of toe irons screwed on to the skis. Heel straps were attached to the toe irons, which went around the heels of the boots and were tightened by snap-over clips. The most difficult task of making the skis was the fitting and screwing on the edges.

Finally I stained the skis and was now the proud owner of a beautiful pair of skis ready to go to the snow on Mt Donna Bung with the Rover Scouts when the snow fell. I could hardly wait for that day to come. Making the skis convinced me that I had certainly selected the right trade, that of becoming a fitter and turner and not a carpenter.

CHAPTER 16

THE TURNERY – COLLEGE AND THE SNOW 1946

My next shift was to the turnery, next door to the tender shop where I was shown a lathe, a very simple type compared to many I had seen in the workshops. I was instructed in its use by a foreman named Tom, who was a great bloke and took me through the construction and workings of the lathe like the one shown below. The lathe spindle contained in the headstock is driven by an electric motor through an adjustable vee belt drive system. On the end of the sturdy, hollow spindle, a variety of devices can be fitted, the most usual being a three jaw chuck, which grips the workpiece firmly.

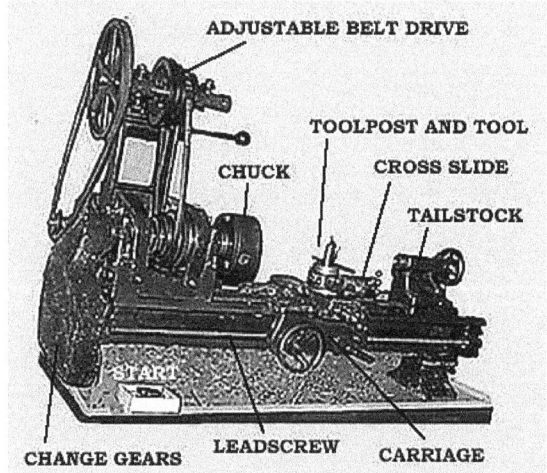

The headstock is mounted on the lathe's bed, a strong casting on which are two machined 'ways' or rails the length of the lathe. Above the ways, and able to be moved along them by means of a hand wheel is the carriage. On the carriage a cross slide, moved by means of a small hand wheel allows for facing and taper turning operations. The tool post in which the lathe tool is clamped is mounted on the cross slide. A tailstock is located on the ways at the far end of the lathe bed. The tailstock enables long items to be turned, by means of a centre in the tailstock, engaging with a centre drill hole in the workpiece and for this use the tailstock can be moved along the bed and clamped in the position required of the work, final movement being made by means of a hand wheel to adjust the tailstock's centre shaft.

I was an apprentice fitter and turner and had done plenty of the first word, 'fitter' in the title of my trade, now I was going to learn about the last word in the title of my trade, turner. Having shown me all of that, Tom then got a square lathe tool and showed me how to sharpen it to the correct shape. He then clamped it in the tool post and showed me how to set the tool at the correct height and position it to make a cut in the solid steel bar in the chuck. Then it was all action, the electric motor was turned on and Tom, having selected the correct spindle speed, asked me to watch carefully as he demonstrated how to turn the workpiece. I watched fascinated as steel chips 'turnings' came from the lathe tool as it progressed along the steel bar. Soon after I had mastered that he showed me how to engage the automatic feed.

Tom said to practice turning various shapes on the workpiece and he would be back later. I had a great time working on the lathe for the next few days as Tom instructed me in the various uses of the lathe, turning tapers and other forms on a workpiece, but I didn't really do any work jobs at that stage. The next project on the lathe was to learn how to cut a Whitworth thread. The thread was to be of six threads to the inch pitch (6 T.P.I.). I recalled simple formulae that I first heard of in College, and which I have never forgotten. The formula is $\frac{\text{LEAD TO BE CUT}}{\text{LEAD OF LEAD SCREW}} = \frac{\text{DRIVER}}{\text{DRIVEN}}$ where the lead to be cut in my case is 6 T.P.I., and the lead of the lathe's lead screw is 4 T.P.I. The driver is the number of teeth of the gear wheel of the lathe's spindle and the driven is the gear wheel needed to drive the lead crew. The ratio between the two is 6-4, so I selected two gear wheels with this ratio, a 30 tooth and a 20 tooth and Tom showed me how to fit them to the lathe. Next using a thread gauge Tom ground a lathe tool to the correct Whitworth angle of 55 degrees and clamped it in the tool post.

Making sure that all was correct to begin cutting a right hand thread, Tom took me through the steps as he cut the thread. After completing that thread, I made another one of the same pitch and then all by myself I made a thread with a different pitch, calculating the change wheels required and fitting them to the lathe to cut the thread. Tom then took me to a modern lathe, which by the use of a number of levers that Tom showed me, made all the adjustments for speeds and feeds that I had carried out manually on the first lathe. At last I was given real turning jobs on the lathe. I was now very pleased because I was now a competent operator of another real workshop machine.

The College half year exams were over and I passed both. Then it was studying the next two subjects for my final year at College. As I remember, the subjects were Applied Mechanics and Trigonometry. I had done well in Trigonometry at the RMTC, but not in Applied Mechanics, so I was a little apprehensive of this subject, however time would tell. In the Trigonometry class we used trigonometry tables to do all our calculations in conjunction with logarithmic tables, as well as all the other calculations that were required, but a slide rule was not to be seen.

Next I was transferred from the lathe to a milling machine learning much the same skills as on the lathes, except that this time it was not the workpiece that was rotating, but the cutter. As on the lathes, I was again under instruction from my foreman Tom. He showed me the workings of the milling machine, its construction and principal parts and set up a cutter on the horizontal arbor and put me to work milling a groove in blocks of steel, although what they were for, he never said. Unlike the first lathe, where I had to apply cutting fluid from a bottle, this milling machine, and the other lathe were provided with a steady stream of fluid from a pump on the machine. Josh, a young, fair headed, tradesman on the milling machine next to me was told by Tom to keep an eye on me as I went about milling the grooves.

The milling machines were close by the large, glass windowed, office of Mr. Jackson the turnery Senior Foreman. One day Josh came over to me and said; "I will show you something funny. Just watch Mr. Jackson and his secretary in the office." So I watched, observing that Mr. Jackson, who always wore a felt hat, had his head bowed over his desk as though he was asleep or dozing. Then as a worker approached the office door, Mr. Jackson's secretary appeared to give a couple of knocks on his desk and Mr. Jackson's head slowly rose and he turned around to look at the person coming in the office door. "Did you see that?" "Yes." I said and we had a little laugh together. While I was working there on the miller I saw the same funny incident many times.

A milling machine, but the bloke on it is not the author

Josh told me that if I had a mower at home, I could bring the cutting reel in and have it sharpened for me in the tool room. I said that would be great as I did the mowing at home, and I was thinking the blades were getting a little blunt. The next weekend I took the mower apart and on Monday morning I took the reel wrapped up tightly in a hessian bag in the train. When I got to work I gave it to Josh. He took me to the tool room a wire enclosed, small workshop and introduced me to one of the toolmakers who said to come and see him on Wednesday, and he will have it sharpened for me. I thanked him and Josh told me that the tool room blokes had hatched up a special job number for sharpening lawn mower blades On Wednesday I picked up the mower reel and the next weekend mowing the lawn, became a much easier task, as the onion weed, was no match for the sharpened blades.

Another day Josh came up to me with a big black book in his hand saying. "This book the *Machinery Handbook* is called the fitter and turner's *Bible. B*ecause I have bought a much later edition, not that there is much difference from this 1919 edition, you can have this one for ten shillings if you like." I had a look at it and was amazed at the information it contained. The name *Machinery Handbook* was embossed in gold letters on the cover of the 2½" thick book. I said thanks and purchased it from him and have treasured it through all the years. I still have it although it is getting a little worse for wear.

Winter arrived and with it snow on the Alps and also on Mt Donna Buang 4,080 ft. (1.240 m), which in those years had reliable, skiable, snow for at least the two months of July and August. However, from that year 1946 until the present year (2025), I estimate that the snowline has risen by about 600ft (183m) and no longer does Mt Donna Buang have skiable snow in the winter. I would like those who do not believe in 'global warming' or 'climate change' to explain to me why this is so.

I was thrilled that at last when one Sunday in July I joined a Rover Scout ski trip to go skiing for the first time on Mt Donna Buang located above Warburton the same town where we began our Easter hike. We travelled very early in the morning by furniture van to miss the crowds, which usually arrived there just before noon. We all had to get out and push the van to the car park at the turntable, as it could not make the last half mile or so through the snow.

The ski run on Mt Donna Buang was quite steep with a good cover of snow. I clipped on my skis and tried walking and doing a basic 'kick turn' as I had practiced on the back lawn at home, but I quickly found out that the snow was not as forgiving as the grass on which to try out my skis. I tried a few slides on a flat section and after a few falls, I plucked up enough courage to point the skis down the run and promptly fell over. Not surprising of course. If at first you don't succeed, try again, so I tried again and again and gradually I became a little more stable on my skis, which worked very well. I was not however, up to their standard of perfection. I took a great liking to the white, cold, substance that fell from heaven having no idea on this day that this new found interest in the sport of skiing would become such a major factor in my life.

On the ski run at Mt Donna Buang, the author is fourth from left
photo by an Argus photographer

In August about two weeks after my first exciting trip to the snow, I went again to Mt Donna Buang on another Rover Scout ski trip and my skiing improved considerably, as I was able to turn at the end of the run instead of falling over, which was a huge benefit. Of course there was no ski tow, so one had to master the art of 'side stepping,' or 'herringboning' to climb back to the top of the run, and I learned on that weekend to perform these actions successfully. I was very pleased that all the ski equipment I had made, the skis, the bindings, the stocks and the improvised ski boots worked well. The program for these Sunday Rover Scout ski trips was to arrive about 10 a.m. and ski before all the crowds came around noon, which made skiing on the run very crowded.

At 2 p.m. we left the run to all the day trippers and climbed into the furniture vans and we were back in the city by about 5 p.m. At the time of writing, the ski run on Mt Donna Buang is now overgrown and when snow does fall there, it is only suitable for sightseeing and snowball throwing, but Donna Buang did a great service to the sport of skiing in Victoria. Many young people like me, who became skiing enthusiasts and lovers of the mountains, gained their first experience of the joys of skiing on Mt Donna Buang.

CHAPTER 17

A RAIL STRIKE – J J BROWN AND A BIKE TOUR 1946

The year of 1946 saw the beginnings of a new war, the 'Cold War,' which was really no more than a weapons race between Russia and the USA. The Communist Party in Australia was making its presence felt much to the chagrin of the leader of the opposition Liberal Party, Bob Menzies, who was trying to have the party banned. The Australian Railway Union (ARU) led by the Communist Secretary J. J. Brown, together with other Communist led industrial unions, began the push for a shorter working week from 44 hours to 40 hours, together with other claims. It was while I was working in the turnery on the milling machine that a series of union, mass meetings began to take place during lunch times. J. J. Brown addressed a couple of these lunchtime mass meetings on a platform erected for the purpose outside the carriage shop.

At first I did not take much notice, but one lunch time instead of reading a book I went and had a look. The union shop steward for the ARU at the workshops was a big bloke by the name of Mr Treasure, who always opened a meeting with a short address before he called on J.J. Brown to speak. J. J. Brown, a well built, red faced, man always opened his address with the word "comrades", which even allowing for its Russian overtones, I felt it to be an appropriate form of address under the circumstances. J.J. Brown was actually the skipping champion of Victoria for quite some time, so despite the red, blood filled face, he was a very fit man. He then went on to speak loudly to an audience of about one hundred employees. Not all of those present were members of the ARU; some would have been tradesmen of various unions, the Amalgamated Engineering Union (AEU) to which most fitters and turners belonged, as well as other unions, electrical, boilermaker and the like. I had in fact been asked to join the AEU early that year, but declined mainly because as an apprentice I was not required to join. Belonging to a union was not compulsory at the Newport Workshops, but my understanding was that the majority of workers in those years saw fit to be a unionist.

After attending one of first of these meetings, where voting was always by a show of hands, I learned two valuable lessons. The first of these was when I picked up a newspaper on the way home on the day of the mass meeting and read the report in the newspaper of the meeting, I found it to be grossly distorted, and bore little resemblance to the conduct of the meeting I had attended that day. From that day on I have always been very wary of the truth of reports I read in newspapers. The other lesson I learnt concerned the apathetic attitude of some of my workmates. After attending a number of these mass meetings and returning to my workplace, I was usually asked; "What happened at the meeting today?" In reply I would give them a short account of the decisions taken at the meeting, which usually engendered a disgruntled response.

I continued going to these 'combined union shop meetings' as they were called, which meant that the vote of those workers who belonged to unions other than the ARU was legitimate. One day when I returned to work after a meeting, I was asked the same question; "What happened at the meeting today?" This time however, I finally got fed up and replied. "Why weren't you at the meeting?" They said that they did not like Communists, to which I said to them, in no uncertain terms for a third year apprentice. "Well go and vote against them." Whether they did or not I was not sure, but they never asked me again. I must admit that to all the motions that were put to the meetings, I don't remember one hand going up to vote against any of the motions.

I think that despite the Communist presence, most workers were in favor of the 40 hour week and other benefits the Communist unions were seeking. Mr. Menzies was Prime Minister of Australia for a short period from 1939 to 1941, but was overthrown and eventually became the Liberal leader of the Coalition and Ben Chifley, a former locomotive driver, became the Labor Prime Minister in 1945. Menzies hated the Communist party and did everything he could to negate their policies and ban the party.

One day the news came through that Mr. Menzies wanted to speak to the workers at the Newport Workshops at noon, but he was not allowed to address the men inside the workshops, so Menzies had to hold the meeting outside the main gates in Champion Road. I wandered out there at lunchtime, where a sort of rostrum had been set up for him to stand on. There was quite a good gathering of men waiting, but he was late, and when he eventually arrived, he stood up on the rostrum and apologized saying he had been held up at the Bendigo Workshops. Immediately someone yelled out. "I don't know why you bothered to come at all!"

Robert Menzies

Menzies, a well-built man with greying hair, was known to be a very fine orator and quick on the repartee. Quick as a flash he answered. "Well, why did *you* come, was it to hear something that might raise your intelligence level, which might be an impossibility for the likes of you?" Or words to that effect. With that he began his speech in his upper class accent to which the men listened in complete silence, not willing to risk another interjection and another equally stinging reply. He spoke about working conditions and a little about the Communists, but he was treading a fine line because in criticising the Communists he had to be careful not to alienate the workers many of whom, although not Communists themselves, had sympathy for the party and of course its fight for better working conditions for all workers. The whistle sounded and we all returned to work, from what I thought was an interesting opportunity to meet and listen to what Menzies had to say, although even at that stage in my life I was not one of his admirers.

Eventually on October 7th in support of claims relating to annual leave, the basic wage, overtime rates and the forty hour week there was a one day strike; another day when I could not get to work. After a couple more mass meetings with J.J. Brown really going to great heights of strident oratory, with his face getting redder and redder all the time, the result was that the meeting voted for strike action. Two weeks later a strike was called and all railway employees, not only the ARU, but the AEU and all the other unions, tramway employees as well, went on strike and all services were suspended for nine days.

I got in touch with Harry Gilham, who like me was not on strike, but could not get to Newport. We decided to go on a bike ride for two days on the 25th and 26th October to Mt St. Leonard (3,283 ft.), which rises to the north of Healesville and is a very prominent mountain peak on the eastern skyline as seen from Heidelberg and Rosanna. It was really good to be able to go on a bike ride together and under cloudy skies we rode our bikes to Healesville by way of

Mt St. Leonard on the horizon

Lilydale, and then camped for the night a short distance along the road to Mt St. Leonard, near where we had once camped with the scouts. The next morning bright and early we started off, but it was no bike ride up to the summit of Mt St. Leonard.

After we left the main sealed road we began to walk our bikes up the very steep, rough, gravel road to the top of the mountain, where we were surprised to see snow covering the final part of the climb to the summit. There was a high fire tower on the summit, but nobody was watching for fires as this was October, but there is no doubt that this was a wonderful summit on which to erect a fire tower, because the view was superb and well worth the effort of the climb. The Yarra Valley lay in the foreground, with Port Phillip Bay and the city in the distance. In the west Mt Macedon could be clearly seen and the nearby Kinglake Ranges, while to the east the Dandenong and Warburton Ranges were in full view.

The fire tower

Mt. Tanglefoot and the firebreak

To the north Mt. Tanglefoot rose along the snow covered fire break. On the steep climb we had contented ourselves with the thought that we would be able to freewheel all the way back down and now it was time to reap that reward, so after taking a few photos we started off back down the rough, steep, track, but it wasn't long after commencing the slow descent with the full braking power of both drum and rim brakes operating that I smelt my rear brake hub getting hot, so I stopped to have a look. To my horror the drum was showing the blue, temper colours of very hot steel. Tempering steel and temper colours being one of the topics I had learnt about in College. I stopped and packed some snow around the drum brake, which made a loud, crackling noise and started off again. The slope gradually flattened out and soon we rejoined the main road. We made our way home through Yarra Glen, so ending a most enjoyable bike tour, which but for the strike we might never have undertaken.

Apart from going on a bike ride every now and again, I filled in the rest of the nine days playing with my trains and doing odd jobs around the house. My father managed to get a lift in a friend's car every day of the strike to his work at Cox Brothers in the city. Most people who worked in the city and other workplaces were able to get to work by car, bicycle, bus and other means of transport.

CHAPTER 18

A GEAR WHEEL – THE STRIKE ENDS AND MR. RICH 1946

The nine day strike came to an end and it was back to work for me in the turnery on the Cincinnati milling machine, where my foreman Tom gave me the job of cutting a gear. Not just to cut an ordinary 50 tooth, spur gear in a cast iron blank, but a much more challenging task that of milling a 128 tooth, helical gear, in a bronze gear blank about 6" diameter and 5/8" wide. This was for the timing gear of a petrol electric rail motor, of the type that I had just discovered that provided a passenger service on the Whittlesea line, and many other country branch lines. I had learned a little about gear cutting at College in the Workshop Practice class, about the type and size of gear cutters used, the use of a 'dividing head' and various types of gear teeth, one of which was helical gears. I had a lot more to learn and my instructors were to be my foremen Tom and the tradesman Josh on the milling machine next to me.

A Cincinnati milling machine
Photo Industrial Surplus

The Cincinnati milling machine that I had been working on before the strike was a very versatile machine, which with its many accessories was able to perform a great variety of milling jobs. I was now going to use it to cut a gear. I helped Tom lift the heavy, dividing head, one of the machine's accessories up on to the milling machine table and bolt it securely to the table. A dividing head is a mechanical device used to positively divide a circle into a number equal divisions or degrees. It consists of an output shaft on which can be fitted a chuck or other attachment to hold a workpiece.

The dividing head has a hand crank handle that rotates the output shaft. The hand crank is connected to the output shaft by gears, with usually with a 40-1 ratio, so that forty turns of the handle will turn the output shaft one complete turn. Permanently attached to the input shaft is an indexing plate that rotates with it. The plate has a series of equally spaced rings of holes of various numbers, 24, 30 and 36 in each row and there is a selection of various plates that can be interchanged with a different selection of hole numbers. A pair of adjustable sector arms is also carried on the index plate and rotates with it. A spring loaded pin on the hand crank engages with these holes.

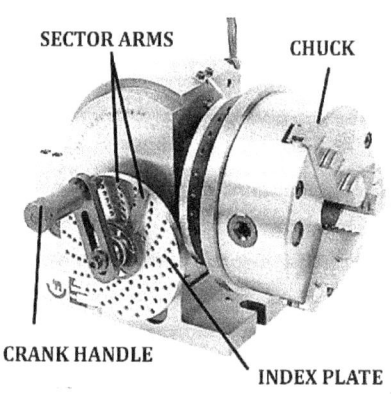

A dividing head showing the main components

The dividing head that I would be using to cut the helical gear was a universal dividing head, which has provision for the output shaft to be rotated as a tooth is cut. This gave the dividing head the ability to cut spiral gears, splines and flutes in reamers and other jobs of a similar nature. Tom said that he had already set up the gear train on the end of the milling machine table, and connected it to the dividing head. He said he would show me later how to do this. The next task Tom said was to set up the dividing head to cut 128 teeth. One way to do this was using a formula or a chart. He said we will use the formula as it would give me a better idea of the working of the dividing head. As the timing gear was to have 128 teeth, I had to find number that would divide into128 and give a whole number. That was easy, 4 gave me the whole number 32, the hole circle number. I then used the formulae: $R = (H \times 40) \div D$, where R is the number of holes between the sector arms, H is the number of the hole circle, 40 is the dividing head gear ratio and D is the number of teeth. The calculation $R = (32 \times 40) \div 128$: results in $R=16$, the number of holes between the sector arms on the 32 hole circle that I would have to select o advance the gear one tooth after I had cut the first tooth.

Tom then helped me set up the dividing head using the results of the two calculations. The phosphor bronze gear blank was then placed on a mandrel with spacers and tightened securely with the nut on the end. This was placed in the chuck of the dividing head and tightened and the other end of the mandrel was located in the tail stock. The correct size gear cutter had been selected for me and this was fitted to the horizontal arbor of the mill, tightened and then centred over the mandrel carrying the gear. Having set the dividing head in the position to make the first cut, Tom started up the milling machine and brought the table up just enough to allow the cutter to make a small cut or 'witness mark' in the blank. He then left me to rotate the gear blank through a full turn using the crank handle and sector arms, to put a cut in the blank about every tenth tooth, until the blank had turned a full circle and the last cut matched exactly up with the first cut I had made. This proved that the calculation, setting and my operation of the dividing head was correct.

Tom then showed me how to operate the machine to cut the first tooth. He made the first tooth cut a few thousands of an inch less than the correct depth and then rotated the dividing head and made the next cut, which produced the first tooth profile. With a set of vernier gear callipers he showed me how to check the size of the tooth. As expected it was not correct, so he raised the milling table by the correct amount and deepened the cut, and after checking with the callipers, he said the gear tooth profile was correct. He said he obtained these measurements from his *Machinery Handbook* and wrote them out for me on a piece of paper. "Do you think you can carry on now and cut the rest of the teeth?" He asked me. "OK I think so," I said not too confidently. He called Josh over and asked him to keep an eye on me and then he was off. Using plenty of cutting fluid on the cutter,

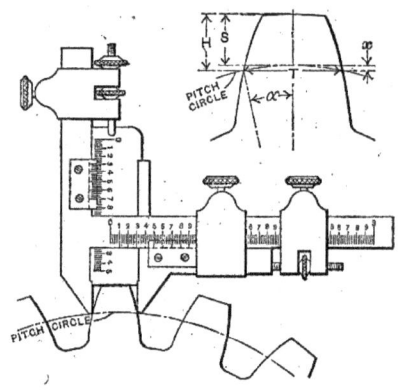

Vernier calipers for checking the size of a gear tooth
Diagram from Machinery Handbook 1919

I carried on cutting the teeth, which of course I found much more exciting than cutting teeth as a small child, but not much faster, because it took me a few weeks from the day I cut the first tooth. Working on cutting the gear was interrupted by having to go to College. How I wished College would end and I could spend all my time working on gear cutting. As I cut the teeth, I made sure that the witness cuts exactly matched as I milled the teeth around the circumference of the blank, and I was very pleased with myself as I approached the cutting of the last tooth, but to my horror, I saw that something was not quite right. I realized that the last tooth didn't line up! I had the choice of finishing up with one large or two small teeth, Ha-Ha. Although I had observed all the necessary precautions in setting up very carefully I wondered what could have gone wrong.

I showed Josh and he couldn't work out why. He had checked me from time to time and everything seemed to be going OK. He said that I better go and tell Tom. So with some trepidation, I sought out Tom to explain my predicament. Trying to make light of it, I jokingly said to him: "I'm sorry, but I have made a mistake cutting the gear wheel, shall I make the last tooth two small teeth, or one large one?" He looked at me in amazement for a moment and said: "Let's go and have a look." Josh came over and said that he had watched over me and it all seemed to be going well. Tom was very kind, he never went off crook at me, but said, that this was the first time I had the experience of cutting a gear on a milling machine and that we had better find out what went wrong. I said that the witness marks had lined up perfectly as I cut the teeth. "Let me have a look" he said as he checked the tightness of the mandrel in the chuck and the gear blank on the mandrel.

Then after some thought and looking at all the set up, he said to me: "It's not your fault Gordon, I omitted to come and see you and take the cutter and have it sharpened about every twenty teeth. Phosphor bronze is quite hard really, and because you were cutting a spiral gear, the cutter tends to push the blank sideways as it cuts. It might only move less than one thousand of an inch with each cut, but after a hundred or so teeth it adds up, but not enough to notice from the witness marks. "Don't worry Gordon we all learn by our mistakes." That was the end of the matter, but I was never the less very embarrassed.

The faulty gear wheel was taken away to be melted down and Tom brought me another blank, which I set up in the milling machine; but before beginning to start work on the new blank I took the cutter off and Tom took me to the tool room and introduced me to a tool maker and asked him to sharpen the cutter for me. "When you get it back and start work cutting another gear, after you have cut the first tooth with the sharpened cutter, check the tooth profile with the calipers and make any adjustment you have to, to get the size of the tooth correct. Then use the calipers to check the tooth size, every ten or so teeth and at the same time retighten the mandrel and the chuck. Also take the cutter off about every twenty teeth and take it to get sharpened. Then check the size of the next tooth you cut. I will leave you with it." So I began repeating the whole gear cutting process again, being careful to carry out all the instructions he had given me. Thankfully about three weeks later with the usual College interruptions, I had completed the gear wheel, which Tom inspected and congratulated me on being able to make a perfect gear wheel. I then went on to less challenging, but still interesting jobs on the milling machine.

One day my father told me he met a bloke on the train by the name of Frank Rich who was a member of the Victorian Model Railway Society (VMRS). My father told him about me being an apprentice fitter and turner at the Newport Workshops and how I had built a model of a Z van, which by showing the model at the interview had helped me being selected as an apprentice. Frank Rich offered to take me into the next VMRS club night. I said that would be really good so very soon my father took me down to the Rosanna railway station to meet Mr Rich, who also lived in Rosanna. I accompanied Mr. Rich on the train into the city where we walked along Swanston Street to the club meeting, held downstairs in the Model Dockyard the shop I was well acquainted with, but it was still a thrill again to be surrounded by all the models.

The meeting was very interesting as various members displayed and talked about the models they had built, which were mainly VR locomotives, in both H0 and 0 gauges. Mr. Rich asked me if I had enjoyed myself at the meeting and if I would like him to take me to the next one in a month's time, and of course I said I would. He said: "Your father has told me about the Z van you built, would you like to show it to the club members at one of the meetings and describe how you built it?" I thought for a moment and said that "Yes I would like to." Mr. Rich said he would arrange it for the month after next, which if I remember correctly would be the January 1947 meeting. I thanked him and looked forward to what would probably my first talk to an audience.

A little after that night I discovered that Frank Rich was a comedian and performed on radio stations with two other comedians Perry and Rowe. In those years they were a very good and popular comedy team, known as Perry, Rich and Rowe. I had heard them many times on the ABC and other radio stations and of course I was elated to discover that Mr. Rich was one of the team.

CHAPTER 19

LEARNING TO OPERATE A GRINDING MACHINE 1946

I continued on working on the milling machine until one day my foreman Tom said to me: "When you have finished that job, let me know because I am going to put you on a surface grinder to learn how to work that machine. A couple of days later, Tom took me over to another part of the turnery where there was a machine very different from a milling machine or a lathe. He said: "This is a Blohm surface grinding machine and seeing you have mastered the operation of the milling machine, let's see how you get on with this one." With that he went through the controls of the grinder, how it operated and what work he wanted me to do on it.

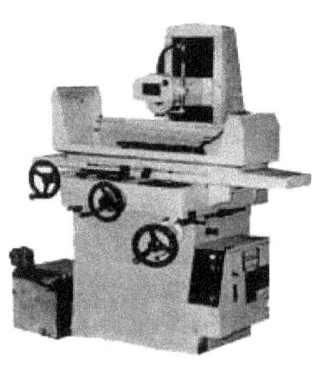

A Blohm surface grinder

The Blohm surface grinder was a pedestal type machine consisting of a base with various controls in the form of hand wheels. Above the base there is a long steel platform on which a moveable table is located. The table has a flat, electro-magnetic chuck bolted to it, and is driven by a low pressure hydraulic power unit located in the base, which moves the table backwards and forwards along its length by means of a long hydraulic cylinder. As well the table can be moved sideways incrementally a short distance. Above the table a grinding wheel about 6" diameter and 2" wide driven by an electric motor is contained in an overhanging integral housing, which can be adjusted for height. The limits of travel of the table can be adjusted by stops.

Tom put a flat bar of steel, which he said was a part for carriage doors on the magnetic table and flipped the switch that operated the electro-magnetic chuck, holding the part securely on the chuck. I was a little amazed that it was held tightly enough to be able to be ground, so Tom said: "Try and move it." I did, but I couldn't budge it. Tom then showed me how the table operated. He moved the small table control lever and the table began to move slowly and nearly silently, backwards and forwards. He controlled the distance it moved by adjusting stops on the platform and then started up the grinding wheel, which spun at a very high speed. Next he showed me how to alter the height of the grinding wheel by means of another control wheel, bringing the grinding wheel down until it just touched the guide, causing a few sparks to be produced. Tom said that the thickness of the part was nearly correct after having been machined roughly to size before surface grinding. What I had to do was to finish grinding them to the correct thickness, first by cleaning up one side, turning it over and grinding the other side to the correct size with the use of a micrometer.

"I will do the first one for you," Tom said and he operated the grinder making the table pass backwards and forwards under the grinding wheel and by turning a tap the grinding wheel was flooded with coolant, so much so that hardly a spark emerged from the wheel. When he had ground one side he undid the magnetic chuck, measured the size with a micrometer saying to me that there was about another 10 thou (thousands) (010") to be taken off it. The thickness he said had to be correct to plus or minus ten thou of the final size. He lowered the grinding head about five thou (005") showing me how to do this by means of graduations in thousands of an inch on the sleeve of the adjustment wheel. Operating the grinder removed this amount and checking again revealed that there was exactly four thou (004") remaining to be removed to bring the part within the correct ten thou. tolerance.

Having done this and after checking that the size of the part was correct he turned to me and said: "It's now your turn, do you think you can do the next one?" I think so, I said. Then he left me saying: "First, operate all the adjustments so that you are familiar with them all and when you are, come and get me and I will watch you while you do the next one". I manipulated all the controls until I reckoned I knew what they did, I went and got Tom and with him watching me, I started up the surface grinder and the grinding wheel, slowly bringing it down on the guide until a few sparks indicated that the wheel had just made contact.

Taking note of the number of the graduation on the height adjustment I backed off the wheel and brought it down a few thou. I turned on the coolant tap and the table control lever and away went the table moving backwards and forwards as the grinding wheel cleaned up the first side. I was still a little dubious that the magnet could hold the guide under the action of the grinding wheel, but soon overcame that fear. I finished grinding the part to the correct size without any problems, so as Tom was satisfied that I could work the grinder OK, left me to get on with it, with a cautionary word to come and get him straight away if I needed help in any way. It felt great! I was actually making something, of course forgetting that I had actually made a gear wheel, but there was no second try this time.

I rather enjoyed working the surface grinder and carried on without problems. In no time at all I had complete confidence in my ability to operate the grinder to the satisfaction of Tom my foreman. There were many parts to be ground and this kept me busy for the next few weeks. I was now proficient at the working of another metal cutting machine in the stable of machines used in my trade. The surface grinder was a good machine to operate, clean, quiet and effortless, the magnetic chuck contributing largely to the holding of the work piece, compared to a chuck on a lathe or the milling machine. One feature of the grinder I did miss however, was seeing the metal cuttings being removed from the work piece in various forms, depending on the machine and the cutting characteristics of the cutting tool. The grinder produced no visible cuttings under the flood of coolant, these only becoming apparent after grinding many guides when they collected on the table in small heaps of grey filings and had to be cleaned up from time to time.

CHAPTER 20

AN OXY-ACETYLENE WELDING CLASS COLLEGE ENDS 1946

I had a break from the grinder for five days when I was notified by Tom, a great bloke that I was to attend a welding class beginning next Monday in the brake shop. On Monday morning I rolled up in the brake shop, where I met not only Kevin and Allan, but also some of the other apprentices that I had met at College. We talked together for a while then a bloke in a leather apron called us all together. He introduced himself as Ken, a youngish bloke who said we were going to learn how to use oxy-acetylene equipment to weld and cut metal. There were a couple of short rows of benches and besides these there were oxy-acetylene bottles with welding torches. I was familiar with some of this equipment because I had seen it being used many times around the workshops. I thought how beaut it would be to learn how to use all this equipment to cut and weld steel.

Ken took us over to a bench with a set of welding gear. He said that we would be working with equipment, which if it was not used correctly could be dangerous, repeating the warning, further saying that welding and cutting steel involves generating very high temperatures, and that burns have to be avoided. First we were shown the items of an oxy-acetylene welding set and their functions. He told us that the pressure regulators and their gauges are attached to the bottles by a right hand thread for the oxygen and a left hand thread for the acetylene, so that they cannot be screwed into the wrong gas bottle. He demonstrated how to set the regulators to the correct pressure for welding 5 psi (pounds per square inch) for the acetylene and 10 psi for the oxygen, and how to read the pressures shown on the gauges, one gauge indicating the amount of gas left in in the gas bottles.

Having provided each of us with a pair of dark goggles he showed us how to light the welding torch and adjust the flame to the correct cone shape. We then all drew a little closer to watch him use the welding torch, as he showed us how to make a pool of molten metal on a piece of mild steel and how to move along with small movements of the torch from side to side making a path of molten metal in the piece of metal as the torch moved forward.

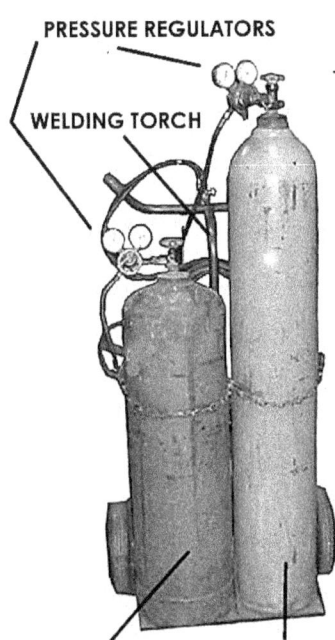

A portable oxygen-acetylene welding set

We were then told to go to one of the benches with a welding set, turn on the gas bottles with the handles, set the pressures and light and adjust the flame. When we had done that, Ken said he will come around to each of us and check to make sure the flame cone was correct. Ken checked my flame and made a small adjustment then left me to begin using the torch to melt the metal. When that was OK I went on using the torch to melt the metal and make runs of melted metal, leaving a mottled pattern of previously molten metal in the plate. It took some doing, but after a few runs I got the hang of it. Ken checked each of us in turn to make sure we had used the torch correctly and mine was OK. When all the class had been checked he went on to the next part of the instruction.

With the addition of a thin welding wire positioned in front of the torch flame, he showed us how to melt the metal as we had just done and melt the end of the welding wire in the pool, then continue as before laying down a slightly raised bead of metal, in the same type of pattern as we had before. I enjoyed doing that exercise and when he was satisfied that the whole class was in control of the procedure, Fred went on with the next exercise. Joining two pieces of metal together in a butt weld; using welding wire. Ken demonstrated this and then left it to us to get on with it, but of course with him overseeing us as he went from bench to bench as we were welding away. At first I found the welding a little difficult requiring some dexterity and good vision through the dark glasses, but at last I had success.

Next there was instruction on the use of the cutting torch where the oxygen pressure was increased to 50 psi. The cutting torch had a flat lever on its barrel, which when operated opened an orifice in the centre of the nozzle allowing a jet of high pressure oxygen to be emitted to cut the steel after it had been preheated. We were shown how to adjust the oxy-acetylene preheating flame surrounding the oxygen orifice of the torch, which did the actual cutting of the steel. The cutting torches were equipped with a device clamped to the body of the torch which kept the torch at the correct distance from the piece of metal to be cut. We were supplied with leather aprons to put over our boiler suits and overalls for this task and then we gathered around Ken as he showed the class how to preheat the edge of the piece of steel to be cut.

As soon as it was just on the point of melting, he turned on the oxygen by means of the lever on the cutting torch and began cutting the steel amidst a shower of sparks and molten metal. He told us that sometimes, on a thick piece of steel, if a cut has to be made, beginning not from the edge of the work piece, but from somewhere inside the piece of steel, to cut a hole for example, it would be necessary to drill a hole in the position where the cut had to begin.

I found that welding metal pieces together fascinating, seeing the molten steel fuse them as one, while cutting steel with the torch was a revelation. I was quite excited knowing that these skills added to my bank of considerable knowledge leading towards my goal of becoming a fully-fledged tradesman. During the hours we spent in the class using the gas welding equipment, Ken took us aside occasionally to describe and explain further information about using oxy-acetylene equipment. The use of cleaning tools to keep the orifices in the torches clean. This being particularly important using the cutting torch, in being able to make clean, slag free, cutting. He showed us a selection of various sizes of cutting and welding tips for heavier cutting and welding jobs.

Lastly it was back to safety. If it was found difficult to screw in the regulator and gauges into the oxy bottle NEVER USE OIL as this could lead to an explosion. Never leave a torch alight and unattended and finally, if either the oxygen or acetylene hoses become worn, or are suspected of leaking, always get them attended to straight away. Finally the week's course came to an end with only two interruptions to attend College. We all thanked Ken who we reckoned had been a good and patient instructor. After completing the very instructive and interesting oxy-acetylene course I went back on the surface grinder.

I went to the November meeting of the VMRS with Frank Rich who said to call him Frank. At the meeting there were a couple of members who described how they built their model locomotives, which of course I found particularly interesting, especially so because with my talk about my Z van coming up in January, I took special notice of the way they spoke, to help me in my talk. It was announced at the meeting that next January the VMRS would be having on display, a model train layout in a model exhibition to be held in the Melbourne Town Hall, so that was something to really look forward to.

    1946 was rapidly coming to a close and so was College. I really enjoyed my time at our excellent College, a facility that very few companies have that take on apprentices. It was certainly a bonus for VR apprentices especially because many of the instructors were VR railway men themselves. The only negative for me about College, and this could certainly not be blamed on the College was that the two half days each week that I spent there interrupted my time in the workshops. I must say however that this was only when I was working with Vic in the erecting shop on the Garratt in my first year. The variety of subjects I studied at College were very good, besides another feature of the VR having its own College was that many of the topics taught in some of the subjects were directly related to railways. There were scholarships to be won to higher education, but neither Kevin, Allan or myself won any of these, nor did any other students that I knew personally, and as it turned out, I was not sorry that I didn't win one. Finally the last day at College arrived and we all shook hands with the instructors, and I said goodbye to a very important period in my goal of becoming a fitter and turner.

    I continued to work on the surface grinder until the day before I knocked off for the Christmas holidays. I wished Kevin and Allan all the best over Christmas and especially thanked Tom for being such a great foreman and instructor for looking after me and guiding me safely through the sometimes complicated learning process on the various machines. The lathes, the milling machine and surface grinder, all of which I was now competent in my ability to operate.

    I was presented with my free railway pass and so the third year of my apprenticeship came to an end.

Towards the end of last year some members of our Rover Crew expressed a desire to visit the Bogong High Plains (BHP) to see some of the country that I had described to them in glowing terms when I came back from the Rover Scout work party in 1945. There was no work party scheduled to the Rover Scout chalet for this year, so we decided to go on a hiking tour to the High Plains ourselves. We discussed the possibilities and finally four of us got together to plan a hike across the BHP. With my help and a lot of map reading, we decided to take nine days for the crossing, which also included climbing the major peaks in the area. The four Rovers Scouts who were able to go were, Harry Gilham, Maxwell Macdonald, Alan Burgess and me. We planned on catching the train on January 10th to Bright and then catch the bus to Harrietville. From there we would climb Mt Feathertop and then make our way via Mt Hotham on to the BHP, finally leaving the BHP to climb Mt Bogong. We would then descend via the Staircase Spur to Tawonga and home again by bus and train. That was the general plan, which we hoped would be without any problems.

The four of us got together on numerous occasions after our decision to go, to decide on the food we would need to take, as well as all the other essentials for the whole nine day hike. This was very necessary as there was no place where we could buy extra food or other requirements during our hike once we left Harrietville. At the time there were various shops in Melbourne that sold a range of dehydrated food, mainly vegetables. These had been developed and used during the last war, so we decided it would be a good idea to purchase some of these, potatoes, carrots, peas, beans, dried eggs and various types of dried meats.

The only tinned food we included was some small tins of condensed milk, fruit salad and camp pie. For breakfast we selected porridge, which I dislike, but it was the most practical breakfast meal, easy to carry and prepare for the first meal of the day. Added to this list were the usual salt, pepper, tea and sugar, as well as plenty of toilet paper, which I was very glad we did as it came in for another quite unplanned use on the hike. We also put together a good first aid kit with plenty of sunburn cream. Each of us had our own sleeping bag, groundsheet-cape, hike tent, torch and we shared a communal set of cooking implements. We had no need to carry any type of stove as there was plenty of dry wood available on the BHP, but we made sure we had plenty of matches, which we carried in a waterproof tin.

At one of our final preparation meetings we divided all the foregoing up between us as best we could. The final weight of each rucksack came out at around 80 pound (36 kg), quite heavy, but manageable, with the knowledge that the weight would diminish slightly with each day we travelled. The only items we had to include on the day was some fruit, apples and smoked cod that we thought would be nice to have as we went along each day.

With regard to clothing, we would be wearing our Rover Scout uniforms and carry one change of underwear, which we reckoned we could wash one set each night and hang it on our rucksacks to dry as we walked along ready for the next day. Most importantly however, we would all be wearing hiking boots that had been *thoroughly broken in*. I remember once on a Scout hike when I wore a pair of new boots. Never again. I had blisters nearly as big as marbles.

CHAPTER 21

ANNUAL LEAVE A NINE DAY HIKE IN THE ALPS 1947

On the morning of Friday 10th January 1947. The four members of our hike met at Spencer Street station and we boarded the train hauled by

The Spirit coming and the Spirit going   a

trusty A^2 to take us to Wangaratta, Alan and Max bought their tickets for the journey to Bright, but of course Harry and I just showed our rail passes to the envy of the other two. I was really thrilled to be going on such a long train journey and I had my head out of the window most of the way. As the train approached Seymour I got a big surprise when I saw the *Spirit of Progress* speeding towards me, however I was very lucky to be able to take a photo of the front and rear of our famous express train as it passed by (as shown on the previous page) on its way to Melbourne, We were having a great time as all four of us had never been on a journey such as this before especially with the sound of the A^2 puffing away up front and its chime whistle.

Over the Great Divide in Seymour we saw *Heavy Harry,* H 220 Australia's largest locomotive and as will be remembered, I had a very close relationship with H 220- intimate one might say-in the first year of my apprenticeship, It was really a thrill to see H220 in action.

H 220 Heavy Harry in Benalla

Looking back on the journey I thought how fortunate I was to see two of Victoria's famous locomotives and get their photos. Our train arrived at Wangaratta around lunch time and we alighted there with our heavy rucksacks, and boarded the train there to take us along the Ovens valley to Bright. It was a lovely sunny day as our train hauled by a K class locomotive choofed its way slowly, but surely along the very, picturesque valley, passing by large paddocks where hops and tobacco crops were growing in abundance.

Porpunkah railway station

Our train stopped at all the stations along the way to load and unload goods, as well as a few passengers here and there. After the train left Gapsted we saw the great, rocky mountain range of Mt Buffalo in the distance. Further along as we approached Porepunkah we were able to observe the gigantic, rock walls of Mt Buffalo and the Buffalo Gorge, a great steep, rocky cleft, which cuts into the north eastern side of the mountain. All to soon because the journey, which had been a beautiful scenic journey along the valley with its picturesque towns, our train came to a halt at the Bright railway station, It was a rail journey that we were able to take that day in our young lives, but sadly not available to travellers today. The railway line has been closed and the track converted to a bike path, which at least is some consolation for present day tourists.

We only had time for a quick look around the beautiful town of Bright, where we managed to buy some smoked cod, fruit, bread and bacon before we caught the bus to Harrietville, further upstream on the Ovens River, deep in the mountains at the foot of the Alps. Just before the bus reached Harrietville, we saw a large machine working on the river flats and we decided to have a look in the morning to see what it was. After a long and exciting day we camped the night in the camping ground surrounded by forested, high mountains on all sides.

We rose early and I had managed to get down my plate of porridge, which certainly filled my stomach and then we went into the small\township of Harrietville a nice little town with a few shops and lots of history. Harrietville is at the beginning of the road that goes up to Mt Hotham and then continues on over the Alps to Omeo. We bought a few postcards and took the opportunity of buying some soft drinks in Harrietville and then we made our way to the Ovens River, where we saw, as well as heard, the huge machine, which had aroused our interest last night. We found it to be massive, floating, gold dredge, dredging the river flats for alluvial gold. It was floating in a large pool that had been dug in preparation for its operation prior to the dredge being assembled ready for use.

The front digging end of the dredge

The control cabin and buckets

The rear tailing end of the dredge

We watched fascinated for a while as a large endless, bucket boom, dug into the working face in front of the dredge, which was gradually pulled both forward and from side to side by large winches that hauled it by wire ropes anchored to each side of the pool. A man controlling the ropes came over to us and asked if we would like to see over the dredge.

Of course we said we would, so he escorted us across a gangway into the dredge's huge, galvanized iron, clad building. He told us it was the biggest bucket dredge in the Southern Hemisphere and had only started operating last year after lying idle during the war. All the operations were powered by electric motors, for which the SEC had erected a power line from Bright especially for the dredge. Inside we saw large revolving screens that contained various size holes, which washed and sieved the material that had been excavated by the buckets. He showed us granules of gold that had been recovered, although to my mind it did not look very much compared to the size of this amazing, noisy, gigantic dredge required to recover it. We could feel the dredge shaking as the buckets bit into the earth.

Our guide then led us from the main dredge building, up a long tailings boom at the rear of the dredge. A conveyor belt ran up this boom, taking the washed material after the gold had been extracted, and deposited the spoil back in the river bed from where it had come, but this time hopefully containing no gold. While we were high up on the tailings boom it swayed like mad and I am sure that if I had stayed up there for too long I would have been seasick.

That was the end of a very informative and unscheduled diversion of seeing over the gold dredge, which aquatinted us with an amazing industry that existed in the foothills of the Victorian Alps. On reflection I doubt if many Victorians knew about gold dredges like this one, which operated in many parts of Victoria. Dredging ceased in Victoria in 1954, as further dredging would have been unprofitable, and a company from Malaya purchased the dredge, for mining tin in that country.

The VR Feathertop Bungalow

After that great experience, we set about finding the track to the Feathertop Bungalow at an altitude of 5000 ft. (1524 m) our objective for the day, which believe it or not, was erected by our employer the VR, as a tourist facility and was equipped with 24 bunks. We found the track without any trouble, but first we had to cross the Ovens River by a bridge about half a mile upstream from where the dredge was operating and that was where we began our wonderful, nine day hike across the Bogong High Plains (BHP) began and from which we did not deviate from our planned route.

*****

Day 10 19th January 1947. The final day of our hike was a beautiful, sunny day. Our hike across the BHP was without any problems at all. We began climbing up the long, high ridge to the east and soon we were on the summit of the highest mountain in Victoria, Mt. Bogong 6,508 feet, which has a large stone cairn on the summit. We took turns climbing the cairn to be the highest person in Victoria, admiring the magnificent long range view in every direction from the summit, extending to Mt. Koscuisko the highest mountain in Australia at 7,328 feet. After we had taken many photos we began the descent of around 4,500 ft. down the Staircase Spur to the valley of Mountain Creek, where we could not help but notice, how hot it now was after spending so long around 5,000 ft, We had a drink and a paddle in the cool, clear water. After drying our feet we divested ourselves of a few clothes and resumed our journey toward the Bogong Hotel.

The summit cairn on Mt. Bogong and the four members of our party

We still had 11 km to go before reaching the hotel, along a rough two-wheel vehicle track, which involved crossing Mountain Creek a number of times at shallow fords. The track was not straight but, infuriatingly it made its way around many rectangular paddocks as it got hotter and hotter. We stopped every now and again and looked back on the long, skyline of the Staircase Spur, a great sight even eclipsing our tiredness and the heat. At last after what seemed

The Staircase Spur in profile

like many hours walking, but was in fact only about two, we came within sight of the bridge over the Kiewa River. As one, we decided that when we crossed the bridge, we would stop for a long rest and another paddle in the river, before tackling the last long slope up a sealed road to the Bogong Hotel.

It was a little bit of Paradise as we went in up to our thighs in the fast running river. Then our minds turned to the thought of cold glasses of lemon squash not far away, so we dried ourselves, slung our rucksacks on our backs and wearily trudged up the road to the hotel, where thankfully we dropped our rucksacks under the shade of a very large deciduous tree in the front of the hotel. We shook hands then fronted the bar, and in no time at all, we had all downed a couple of glasses of lovely, cold lemon squash. Thirst satisfied, we booked in for the night and dinner and were shown to our rooms.

The Bogong Hotel at Tawonga

After an exhilarating shower and clean up, we climbed on to a proper bed and enjoyed the bliss of relaxing and not having to think too much about the next day. Was it all worth it? Of course it was. Six a'clock closing was still the rule, so after we had a rest, we went around to the bar again, where we had another lemon squash with the locals who were quite a varied lot. They were not very interested in us, only how much beer they could consume before 6 a'clock closing time. I saw one character leave the hotel and stagger down the road, only to be bundled into a passing car that dropped him back at the hotel where he resumed his drinking. The stuffed trout, which were displayed around the bar walls, together with the large tree out the front, were the main features of this picturesque Bogong Hotel, which is not in Bogong, a village in the Kiewa Hydro Electric Scheme, The Bogong Hotel is in Tawonga on the Kiewa Valley Highway. After a succulent mixed grill we retired to our beds, with a request to the hotel keeper to wake us up in time for breakfast to catch the bus to Albury.

Day 11 20th January 1947. We were roused early the next morning in time to have a filling breakfast of Kellogs Cornflakes and bacon and eggs, before taking the bus to Albury along the beautiful Kiewa Valley. I looked behind the bus on numerous occasions to see the summit ridge of Mt Bogong on the skyline, growing smaller in the distance, until just before Dederang, where it disappeared from view. Our bus went through Wodonga and over the Murray River into Albury in NSW, the first time I had been interstate.

When the bus arrived at the Albury railway station, we had about an hour to wait for our train to Melbourne. The other three went to have a look at Albury, while I stayed around the Albury station photographing some big locomotives of the NSW railways. I did not think they looked as impressive or as clean lined as our elegant 'A^{2}s' and 'D^{3}s', especially compared to one of our streamlined locomotives 'S 300' *Mathew Flinders,* which just happened to be there. Around noon, we climbed aboard our

Two C 38s of the NSW Railways

stopping train to Melbourne, hauled by an A^2, which brought us into Spencer Street in the early evening. We caught the train to Heidelberg and parted there after shaking hands with each other, after nine days of enjoyable companionship. My next train to Rosanna was not for another 30 minutes, so I elected to walk home, where I received a great welcome from my family, especially from my dear mother, who was so pleased to see me safely home. She straightaway put on my favourite meal of grilled lamb chops and potatoes.

CHAPTER 22

THE DRAWING OFFICE – EDITHVALE AND RAIL STRIKE 1947

It was really great to be back at Newport refreshed after the long hike with wonderful friends. I went back working on the surface grinder, but only for a couple of weeks before I was told to report to the Senior Draftsman in the clock tower. It was quite a change to be in an office environment with a range of large, drawing boards lined up against the side of one large room. The Senior Draftsman Jeff told me that I would be with him for about six weeks learning how to use a drawing board and the various drawing instruments. He said that if I liked working on a drawing board and was interested in engineering drawing, as a branch of my trade, I could take on further studies.

I was given a drawing board to work on and shown how to trace drawings on transparent paper laid over an original drawing, so that the tracing could be used to copy the original drawing. The work was clean with no need for overalls or washing my hands at each break and I quickly became proficient at tracing drawings. The drawings I traced were of all sorts of railway drawings, parts of locomotives, wagons and many other interesting objects some quite large. I learned the difference between 'first and third angle projection' two different methods of drawing views of objects. The drawings I was tracing were in 'third angle', which at the time was the Australian standard and the words 'third angle' in small print were shown, together with the title and other information on the bottom of the drawing. Mistakes in construction of an object are possible, if the object is not symmetrical in all respects and the object is constructed with reference to a drawing of the wrong 'angle'.

The workshop's medical centre, which I had visited on numerous occasions to get a foreign body out of my eye and other minor injuries, was next to the canteen. I often went to the canteen to get a pie or soft drink, and I was usually served by a very attractive, brown haired, young girl about my age called Maree. I was earning a little more money in my fourth year, and I thought I might ask her for a date, the first time I had ever contemplated such a thing. Over a couple of weeks I plucked up enough courage and one lunch time I asked her if I could take her to the pictures one Saturday, but she declined my offer. I tried on a few more occasions with the same result, so I finally gave up.

In early January there was a model exhibition at the Melbourne Town Hall where a wonderful, exciting display of all sorts of working models was exhibited. The VMRS had a very realistic layout based on Anderson railway station and yard on the Wonthaggi-Inverlock line. Most surprising of all was that my friend from the VMRS Frank Rich, using a microphone and loudspeaker behind the display made all the accompanying sounds of the locomotives and rail cars that ran through the layout.

Just after the exhibition and before we went on holidays to Edithvale again, the day came for the January meeting of the VMRS. Frank Rich, my very talented friend met me at the station and with my Z van in a box, we went to the Model Dockyard. After another member gave a speech on building a VR locomotive a D^3, if I remember correctly. It was then my turn. I stood in front of the shop's counters and described the building of my van to about thirty club members. I thought I made a good speech and after answering a few questions, I was given a good round of applause. On the train on the way home, Frank complimented me on my talk, saying it was good.

Being with my family on holiday at Edithvale brought a very busy end to January 1947 with only one regret; Maree would not go out with me. Continuing on with my time in the drawing office, which I quite enjoyed, I found that I was very good at printing, not only copying printing on the tracing paper, but I was also given exercises drawing views of simple objects, using third angle projection, dimensioning them and printing in the titles and other notes. This was not new to me as I had done much the same in Francis William Tough's class at the RMIT.

Our Rover Scout crew received a letter from Rover Scout headquarter requesting that any Rovers who wished to join a party to stay and ski at the Rover Scout Chalet in August, to put in an application forthwith. We discussed it amongst our crew, but only myself and Harry Gilham applied for a place in the party. Then we just waited to see if we were successful.

My six weeks in the drawing office came to an end and although I had enjoyed very much the experience of drawing on a drawing board, it did not give me any thoughts that I would like to be a draftsman after I had completed my apprenticeship, as I found it was a bit too academic and sedentary for my liking. About the same time Rover Scout headquarters notified us that Harry and I had been successful two join a party going to the Rover Scout Chalet for two weeks on the 9th to 23rd August 1947, so we were very happy. Harry Gilham and I went separately to see the Apprentice Master Mr. Curtis, and we both got permission to have our holidays then instead of at Christmas. I am sure that Harry like me, walked away from Mr. Curtis's office with a big smile on his face. I was ecstatic that I was going to see what the BHP looked like under a mantle of snow.

My next move after the drawing office was to the erecting shop, which made me very pleased especially as Kevin was there too. Allan, Kevin said, was at the Jolimont Workshops. Vic King was not to be seen. I was told he had been transferred to North

Melbourne locomotive depot for six months. I began working on a C class locomotive undergoing an A to E examination and I helped installing various cab fittings, the regulator, fire box doors and the like. It was very satisfying to be working on one of the VR locomotives that I had admired so many times before I became an apprentice. It was especially pleasing too, not to have my work days interrupted by the need to attend College.

Quite often during the lunch hour J. J. Brown was back again conducting strident mass meetings with demands for the 40 hour week, better pay and other improved conditions. It appeared that after the strike in 1946 engineering unions in some industries continued on with the strike, but I was unaware of this. However, members of other unions went on strike in sympathy with them, and on April 14th employees were withdrawn from the railway's, power station at Newport, which resulted in the loss of power for the whole suburban train system and all suburban trains ceased to run. This of course meant that once again, I could not get to work and I mucked around at home for a few days.

Knowing that there was a small engineering shop called Georgian Engineer in Heidelberg not far from home, I got on my bike and went and saw the manager. I told him that I was a fourth year apprentice fitter and turner with the VR and could not get to work. Could he give me a job? He said yes. I could work for him while the railways were on strike, so I started there the following day. Georgian Engineering was run by two beaut blokes, George and Ian, which was where the name of their business came from. Believe it or not, I was put on a small lathe, screw cutting a 14" long, square thread, table adjustment screws for small wood worker's tables. That was no trouble as I had already screw cut in the turnery last year, but not a square thread. The method was the same, only the tool shape was different. Everything stopped for morning smoko's when George and Ian listened intently and with much mirth to a soap opera that was on the radio. I couldn't help, but take an interest in the events of the show, but not to the same extent as George and Ian. I enjoyed working there for the whole time of the strike that at last ended on May 8th a total of twenty five days. There was a little talk about whether I might like to remain with them and finish my apprenticeship there, but I said no thanks and after thanking them for taking me on, they said that they had been happy with the time I spent with them.

So it was back to Newport and work as usual, but there was no indication from the government that the union's claims would be agreed to. I went back working on the C class helping to fit all manner of parts including the brake gear, coupling rods, but not the connecting rods or any of the other motion gear because George said it had to be 'blown down' first. Whatever that meant I wasn't sure, but I was about to find out, when one day we all stopped work on the locomotive while it was towed out to the front of the shop by a crane locomotive, which was uncoupled and backed away.

A C class in the erecting shop
A drawing by Robert Emerson Curtis.
Image courtesy of Athur Spartarlis Fine Art

The C class minus all its pistons, smoke deflectors and many other items was then fired to get up a full head of steam ready for being blown down. Eventually when full steam pressure had been built up we were all moved back well away from the locomotive as the Senior Foreman got up in the cab, blew the whistle and opened up the regulator. The result was a loud, ear drum bursting noise as tremendous, tornadoes of steam **at**

200 PSI roared out of both ends of the valve and main cylinders enveloping the locomotive in clouds of steam. The blow down procedure was an awesome event and sight to witness and it demonstrated to me very dramatically the power of high pressure steam and how it is put to work in a locomotive to haul long trains of goods and people and for many other applications.

The author's simulated image of how the C class looked during the blow down

A blow down was always done during an A to E examination after all the work had been completed on the steam passages connecting the regulator valve to the driving cylinders, to blow out any scale or foreign objects left there such as nuts and bolts, or even a spanner maybe. After the blow down it was back to work on the C installing all the motion gear, smoke deflectors and many other items.

CHAPTER 23

SKIING WITH THE ROVER SCOUTS 1947

As winter drew closer I was applying many coats of black Dulux, gloss paint to the running surface of my skis, sanding lightly between each coat. I then left them for a week to dry between each coat. This resulted in a fast and durable running surface. Winter 1947 began with good snowfalls, both on the Alps and on Mt Donna Buang. In late July I went on a ski trip to Donna Buang with the Rover Scouts, which convinced me that the army boots I had converted for skiing would not stand up to a fortnight's skiing on the Bogong High Plains (BHP). A boot maker in Brunswick was making and supplying the Antarctic Division with ski boots so I purchased a pair at quite a reasonable cost. In no time at all Saturday 9th August the beginning of my winter ski holiday came about and I met the Rover Scouts in our ski party of eighteen on Flinders Street station.

We caught the morning train to Bairnsdale, hauled by an elegant A^2. The train carried us swiftly along to the melodious click, click of 30 yard length rails, a sound not heard very much nowadays. At Sale the A^2 was detached and replaced by a smaller, perky, D^3 locomotive, which hauled us the remainder of the journey to Bairnsdale, where we had a pie at the refreshment rooms before boarding a bus to take us to Omeo. Our bus was a 'side loading' coach, like a stretched car with bench seats one behind the other and doors on one side only. The journey through Bruthen and along the

Tambo River was very exciting as the coach made its way around many sharp curves above the rapidly, flowing river. We passed through the saw milling towns of Ensay and Swift's Creek, after which the countryside opened out to rolling plains until we reached Omeo, a distance of just under 200 miles (320 km) from Melbourne. We spent the night at the Hilltop Hotel, which as the name implies is on the top of the hill on the main street.

The next morning we rose early and after a big breakfast we climbed aboard our coach. The dirt road was very narrow as it wound its way along, crossing many creeks on narrow bridges. The country became more timbered and the hills higher and in a couple of places the curves on the road were so sharp that the coach had to go backwards and forwards, to get around them. After a very slow 20 miles we came to the quaint and famous hotel at Angler's Rest, the Blue Duck on the Cobungra River. Leaving the Blue Duck, our coach continued on the winding, narrow road, until we branched off on a track to the left, which opened out to flat grassland surrounding Fitzgerald's property, a very old pioneering and grazing family of this district.

Members of the family enthusiastically welcomed our leader, Bill Waters the Rover Scout Commissioner. Bill was a respected and longtime friend, not only of the Fitzgerald's, but also of many other grazing families in the North East Alpine districts. Our skis, rucksacks and other provisions were loaded on to packhorses led by much loud swearing from one of the Fitzgerald's sons. We then set out along the valley of Middle Creek. Climbing all the time we finally came to the snow line where the snow was too deep for the packhorses to go any further. Our skis and rucksacks were unloaded and we collected them and climbed up in deep snow, filled gully, finally arriving at the Rover Scout Chalet, half buried in snow, where my two week's holiday in the snow really began. I had a wonderful two weeks learning to ski on literally mountains of snow, going on ski tours with our party on the High Plains, but too soon the two weeks came to an end and it was back to work.

Digging out the Chalet the morning after we arrived

A composite photo of the Rover Crews enjoying lunch during a ski tour of Sun Valley at the western end of Rocky Valley on the Bogong High Plains

CHAPTER 24

THE 40 HOUR WEEK IS DECLARED AND AN X CLASS 1947

I went back to work with a nice suntanned face, which surprised my workmates particularly Kevin and George my fitter mate and went back working on the C class, which was just about complete after it's A to E examination. One of the attachments on the side of the locomotive that had a particular interest for me was the cross compound air compressor that made that entrancing, sonorous, panting sound when a locomotive is at rest. The cross compound air compressor generates compressed air for the brakes and other uses. It consists of two mechanisms, a two stage steam engine, integral with a two stage air compressor. It is a very efficient and compact device fitted to large locomotives, which haul long, Westinghouse, safety brake, equipped trains. Smaller locomotives are fitted with a direct acting steam driven compressors.

A C class cross compound air compressor.

I helped with the finishing touches, putting on the smoke deflectors, nearly the last parts to be fitted and I remained with the C class until it was finally steamed up and driven from the erecting shop to take its place hauling heavy good trains on the VR.

The great amazing spectacle and loud noise of the blow down was still in my mind and now I was hearing a very puzzling noise coming from above me, a noise that I heard only every now and again. It appeared to be coming from overhead and as I looked up I saw one of the big, 75 ton, overhead cranes banging itself repeatedly against the crane rail buffers at the end of the shop. I couldn't understand what this was all about until George came to my help, explaining that over time the 75 ton and the 20 ton cranes begin to run crab-wise along the rails. To overcome this problem the drivers run the cranes into the buffers at the end of the shop, until the cranes are moving at right angles to the rails again.

About this time I noticed that most of my fellow fitters could read the time on the large clock at the far end of the erecting shop, whereas I had to walk up closer before I could do this. When I mentioned this to George he said. "You better go and see an optician." I took his advice and went to see Coles and Garrard (C and G), one of the best known optical firms at the time in Melbourne. Their shop was located in Bourke Street just up the hill from Elizabeth Street, so I went there and had an eye test that showed that I was slightly short sighted. I was shown various types of frames and stupidly chose rimless, frames, like I had seen actors wearing in the movies, thinking egotistically that they would not mar my good looks. A week later I went and picked up the glasses at C and Gs. The optician put them on and adjusted them and said; "Look across the other side of the road." I did as he told me, and what a literal revelation it was, the shops on the other side of the road, looked crystal clear without any blurring. I was ecstatic. Unbeknown to me at the time there was another faculty of mine that had begun to deteriorate. My hearing, caused mainly by the loud noise level in the erecting shop, especially the loud noise of rivet guns being used nearby. Not even the boilermakers using rivet guns in the erecting shop putting patches on the frames of A^2s and such jobs wore ear protection, and they used the rivet guns quite near to where I was working. I had not however, spent any time really in the boiler shop to see if ear protection was in use there, but from memory I do not think it was. The boiler shop as I had discovered on my visit there with Vic was a workplace where there was always a veritable cacophony of loud noise from rivet guns and the like.

On the morning of September 9th 1947 *The Sun News-Pictorial* had the following headline emblazoned across its front page:

UNION SATISFACTION AT 40-HOUR WEEK

In a text box below the headline were the following words: *Trade union leaders generally expressed satisfaction yesterday with the 40 hour week decision, announced by the Arbitration Court to operate from the first pay period in January. Employers' [sic] organizations said they accepted the Court's decision and would loyally abide by it, but they emphasized that increased costs would have to be borne by the public.* There was lot more on the front page about the decision, but those words were the most pertinent.

The railway union and other workers here at Newport and elsewhere led by J.J. Brown, had won the long fight and all the mass meetings had served their purpose. In my apprenticeship so far I had learnt about the many facets of a working life in the railways and more. Most importantly the truth of the slogan **'in unity there's strength'**, demonstrated to me by winning the war and winning the 40-hour week. I had learned not to trust what is written in newspapers and the apathy of some workers when moves are made by unions, Communist or not, to better their working conditions. All of this was a part of learning about life that provided for me a good background for the path my life would take me in the future as I re-edit this book to the age of 98.

At last the C Class was ready to be fired and steamed up. When full steam pressure had been reached, under its own power and with release cocks issuing jets of steam it was driven out of the erecting shop, where it was united with its tender. Some time later its driver and fireman came and took it up to the North Melbourne locomotive depot to be further checked, (maybe with the help of Vic King), ready to be put into service hauling heavy goods trains. The C class was a locomotive that I had come to admire, seeing one on many occasions, battling against the odds to start heavy goods trains at Newport while I was waiting for College to begin.

George and I were transferred to work on an X class that I had seen out in the yard and which had just been pushed into the shop by a crane loco and parked over the pit where the C class had been. The X class was so much more immense than the C class, mainly because of its booster trailing truck. For the first time, I was to descend into the pit under the locomotive with George and other fitters to begin removing everything that was connected to the boiler, cab and cylinders, so that the boiler could be lifted clear, leaving only the wheels, coupling rods, pony truck and the booster trailing truck, all of which were to be examined and any work required attended to. I helped remove the horn keepers, parts of the brake gear and then we climbed out to help other fitters remove the connecting rods and some parts of the valve gear.

When this had been completed the two 75 ton overhead cranes came into position and Snow the rigger placed the heavy lifting tackle around the smoke box. Then with a special, spreader lifting rig, he hooked this up to the frame below the cab. Very carefully with the Senior Foremen and fitters watching closely, while I stood back and watched, the top part, which I will refer to as *the boiler etc.* for short, was lifted clear of its wheels and taken down to the far end of the shop where it would be inspected and maintained by other fitters and boilermakers.* See book cover drawing.

A few fitters worked disassembling parts of the booster and it was taken away somewhere to have done whatever was necessary to bring the booster back to working order, while George and I together with other fitters removed the coupling rods, which only left the wheels and their axle boxes. We removed the axle box bearings and these together with the coupling rods, were sent across to the other side of the workshops to be re-metalled, which I guessed was probably done in the small brake shop, where I scraped the bearings. All the wheels were lifted and put on wagons and taken over to the turnery by a crane loco to be put on a wheel lathe and have the tyres reprofiled. George said a couple would need to have new tyres fitted.

This left us with not much to do, so for a couple of weeks we went down and assisted other fitters who were working on the cylinders and valve gear of the X class boiler and a few other minor jobs on other locomotives. I very quickly discovered that I had made the wrong choice of frames for my new glasses. They did not seem to be the right choice for a fourth year apprentice, working on the maintenance of large, steam locomotives, because I broke them and had to go into C and G to have them repaired. After that I looked after them much more carefully and never broke them again.

After all the X class wheels, bearings, the booster and coupling rods had been overhauled, George and I went back to help put them all back together ready for the boiler to be brought back to make one big, working locomotive again. It wasn't very long after we had completed our work that work on the boiler too was finished, and was lifted and placed carefully in the correct position above the wheels, booster and pony truck.

Bringing the two sections back together was quite an exciting and rather frightening experience for me. Together with George and other fitters, we were stationed in the pit, one each to a wheel and its axle box, as well as other fitters watching the booster trailing truck and the front pony truck, to guide the boiler down on to its wheels.

There were also other fitters on the outside, to check that everything was in place as the boiler was being lowered. It was our job in the pit to take hold of the spring hangers, two to each spring and guide them into the spring end cups until they were finally seated. It was rather frightening for me as our rigger Snow, with hand signals directed the crane drivers above, to slowly lower the boiler down, making sure that axle boxes, booster and the pony truck were positioned correctly. I hung on to my two spring hangers carefully guiding them into the spring cups as the boiler was slowly lowered. I got a hell of a fright when there was a big bang and a couple of sparks from a spring hanger next to me as the weight came on and the hanger, not quite in the centre of its cup seated itself as the load was taken up by the elliptical springs. There were a few more bangs and sparks as the boiler finally settled on the frames and the cranes were relieved of their load. We all climbed out of the pit to see the result of our efforts, a locomotive still devoid of most of its motion and valve gear, but looking much more like an X class. *See front cover sketch*

The next job was to finish all the work on the X class necessary to make it a complete locomotive, one of the most powerful and impressive of all of the locomotives in the VR locomotive stable locomotive that I used to admire coming from the football at Essendon. It was standing just outside Spencer Street station on one of the multiple tracks there with a long goods train behind it waiting, I reckoned for its turn to go to Bairnsdale I thought as it was facing in that direction. It was a regular scheduled train too, because I saw the same sight many times, and here I was working on one! Still with George I helped to put it all back together again, the valve and main cylinder pistons, the Walschaert valve gear, the motion gear, the brake gear and all the other connections to the cab. The valve gear was adjusted a little the same as it had been done with the Garratt and after about a month the X class was ready to be steamed up and driven out of the shop.

This fourth year of my apprenticeship was the best, working without College interruptions and mostly working in the erecting shop on big locomotives that had been an object of my admiration in the days before I became an apprentice. After the X class I worked with George on an A^2, but that was only for about a week, before I got a note to tell me that I was to report to Senior Foreman Bill Jamison at the Jolimont Workshops in Batman Avenue on Monday 1st December at 7.30 a.m., and that I would be there for approximately two months.

I thought that maybe the reason for the shift was that as I already had my annual leave and there was probably more work going on at Jolimont than at Newport. So at the end of the week I said goodbye to all my workmates in the erecting shop George, Kevin and a few more, hoping that after the two months was up, I would be back at Newport to finish the last year of my apprenticeship. Working at Jolimont certainly had some advantages, I would not have to get up so early, nor would my mother, who still insisted on getting up to send me off to work. Not only that I would also get home a little earlier.

I was still attending and enjoying the monthly meetings of the VMRS, I was not doing much with my model railway. I had not made any more models and was only running it every now and again, but my other two brothers Donald and Geoff now 15 and 5 years of age respectively were taking a bit of interest in it that pleased our father very much.

CHAPTER 25

THE JOLIMONT WORKSHOPS AND ELECTRIC TRAINS 1947

Monday December 1st 1947, saw me catching the 6.48 a.m. train from Rosanna on which there were many more passengers than on the 6.10 a.m. This train gave me adequate time to walk from Princess Bridge station, across Princess Bridge and down Batman Avenue to the Jolimont Workshops situated a few cricket pitch lengths along the Avenue just short of the Olympic Pool. I found the foreman Bill Jamison, who gave me a friendly welcome and introduced me to a fitter called Harry, who I was to work with. First of all Harry said; "We'll take a walk and I will show you what we have here at Jolimont and I am sure you will find it a lot different to Newport. When we have finished you will be with me working for a while on pantographs."

He took me first to the maintenance workshop, a low, saw tooth, long building with

The carriage maintenance workshop
photo courtesy of AHRS

three, rail over pit bays each able to fit four carriages end to end. Above there were two overhead cranes of about 20 ton capacity, but the driver's cabin, unlike those in the erecting shop at Newport, was not to one side of each crane, but was integral with the crane's hoisting gear and the cabin moved sideways across the crane's gantry. Harry said that much of the minor work, brake block changes, running gear repairs and adjustments were carried out in the Jolimont rail yards, and it was only when this was not practical that carriages were brought into the workshops.

Next he took me to another large section of the workshops adjacent to the main workshops in which pantographs, motors, bogies and brake gear for the carriages were cleaned and overhauled. There were many machines there lathes, millers, grinders and the like, but I don't remember seeing a wheel lathe, I think that wheels when they needed to be turned were sent to Newport. There was also a paint shop and a corner where upholstery and seats were repaired. Last but not least I heard the strange rumbling sound that I first heard at Newport and saw steam rising from the 'witch's brew,' the caustic tank where parts were immersed to clean them of all their grime and grease. After that interesting tour Harry took me back to where he was working on a pantograph, set out with others on a long bench and showed me how he was replacing the worn, copper-graphite, pans that picked up the power from the overhead catenary.

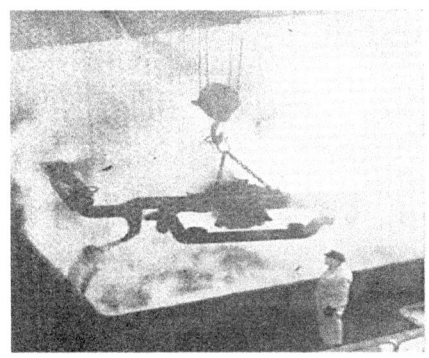

The caustic cleaning tank
Photo VRBTRC

Harry asked me a little about myself and how I was enjoying being a railway apprentice. I told him it couldn't be better. I also told him about me skiing on the BHP and how I was sent to Jolimont because Newport had no work for me over the Christmas holidays.

Harry said that Jolimont never stops working at Christmas and that workers here stagger their holidays, so that was why I had been sent to Jolimont. Harry went on to show me how the pantograph worked. A compressed air cylinder was used to enable the pantograph to be raised and held against the catenary wire by springs and lowered and latched in the down position. I enjoyed working on the pantographs although it tended to be dirty work mainly because of the graphite, the same graphite contained in cast iron. After we had finished overhauling a pantograph and before we moved on to the next one, we tested it with compressed air to make sure it went up and down smoothly and latched when it was lowered. When I looked at pantographs on the top of electric trains, I now knew much more about them and that was quite satisfying. I recalled how I been enthralled in my youth when riding in the guard's van, watching the overhead catenary move from side to side insuring that the wear on the pantograph's pan was distributed evenly over its full width.

Some lunch times I decided if the weather was nice I would sit on a seat beside the Yarra and eat my lunch, then go for a short walk along its banks. As soon as a hot, summer's day came along, I was looking forward to maybe having a swim in the Olympic Pool behind the workshops. I also took walks around the workshops at lunch hours and sometimes I would have my lunch just sitting looking over towards the MCG watching trains go by, especially exciting when I saw a steam train. I soon had a good idea of the amount of work required to service the VR's fleet of electric trains, composed of a mix of swing door and Tait carriages, which seemed to be in a majority and newer than the swing door carriages. There was no doubt however, which was the most comfortable to ride in and *sleep* as I was prone to on many occasions on my early morning journeys from Rosanna to Newport.

I discovered that the Jolimont Workshops looked after a few other items of powered rolling stock besides electric trains or 'sparks' as they were called, parcels vans, two types of electric locomotives, steeple and box and petrol electric rail motors (PEs). On many occasions I would see one of these types of electric locomotives hauling local goods trains and shunting in goods yards at Ivanhoe and Heidelberg. I often saw them too hauling trains of wagons filled with paper pulp along the branch line across Heidelberg Road into the Alphington paper mills. This branch line that left the Hurstbridge line at Fairfield was originally part of the Outer Circle Railway.

Just before Christmas Day I received an envelope from Newport containing the voucher for my new suburban rail ticket, but not of course my free yearly holiday rail pass, because I had that from my winter holiday. When I bought my new suburban first class rail ticket, I got it for Newport Workshops, not just to Princess Bridge. I had four days holiday at Christmas as Christmas Day fell on a Thursday, when we had a scrumptious, Christmas dinner roast, cooked by my loving mother, which was consumed with great pleasure with all the family present. After Boxing day it was Saturday and Sunday, so I didn't go back to work at Jolimont until Monday 29th and then only for a few days, but really, no one was in much of a mood to work very hard. Then it was New Year's Day.

CHAPTER 26

YEAR 5 APPRENTICESHIP AND 40HR WEEK BEGIN 1948

It was not until Monday January 5th 1948 that work for me at the Jolimont Workshops really began again, and I wondered how much longer I would be staying here, but they did say six months. Really I didn't mind, the sort of work I was doing, involved a great variety of fitting, machining and assembling parts of electric trains, even working fitting door handles and window parts to carriages. Most of the work was clean except sometimes when I worked on parts of trailer bogies that had not been through the caustic tank. The blokes too that I worked with were a great lot. They seemed more relaxed than those at Newport as I remember, but why this was so, I was not sure.

One day a fitter I hadn't met before came and asked me if I would like to come with him while he tested a petrol electric rail motor. "Thanks I certainly would," I quickly replied. He took me out to the far end of the workshops where there was a PE rail motor one of a type that I had seen every now and again. I not only liked the look of it, but the rumbling noise of its engine. There were a couple of other blokes on board the PE., and I climbed into the driver's compartment, which was very cramped, because of the big round bulk of what they told me was the 'exciter' for the electric motor of the petrol-electric drive system took up a lot of space. I wondered afterwards who thought up that somewhat erotic term for it. I didn't quite understand at that time that the exciter produced the power for the field windings of the electric motor, but it made a nice warm seat for me as the driver moved the PE away from the workshops and on to a stub siding that came to an end at buffers above Punt Road. After running the PE up and down the line testing the brakes and other tests, the PE was brought to a stop and the engine shut off.

A petrol electric rail motor
Photo VRCEPP

Straight across the main, suburban lines, from where the PE was parked, the sound of cheering could be heard and my workmates said that we were going to climb on to the roof of the PE to watch the cricket. There could not have been a catenary above the test track because if there was, there was no way we would have climbed on to the roof of the PE. One after the other we hoisted ourselves on to the roof and then I could see why the fitter had parked the PE in that particular position. We had a view (not a very good one however) through a gap in the grandstands and could see some cricket being played. It was the 5th test between India and Australia and was actually a 'dead rubber', because Australia had already won three with one match drawn. At that time there were two test matches played at the MCG. Then having seen a little-very little actually-of the action we all climbed down and the PE was driven back to the workshops. I thanked my mates for taking me along with them and providing me with a standing room view of the cricket, which by the way Australia won by an inning and 177 runs. Bradman retiring hurt. Whenever I had seen a PE I loved the throaty, rumbling sound, the petrol engine made, and now I had been up close to the engine and seen where that delightful sound came from. It had been an exciting experience for me.

After my experience with the electric motor exciter, I thought I should learn a little more about the electric motors that drove our sparks, so I took a walk to the section to see where all the electric 'traction motors' the correct term, were and what they looked like and whether they too, had exciters, which in fact they didn't, because they were driven directly with DC power from the catenary. I saw a big lathe turning part of one of the motors and I asked the turner what it was he was turning? With a wry smile he looked at me saying; "It is a commutator–not a communist!" We had a bit of a laugh and a few words together before I moved to have a look at the large, traction motors, where its big gear wheel it meshed with the smaller gear wheel on the axle, and all fitted comfortably into the bogie. These were the gears that when in my early young life we used to travel second class and in the guard's van with my mother, we could feel and hear them grinding away beneath us as the train accelerated. There were other motors that drove the compressors and other electrical equipment overhauled in that section. Seeing all that gave me a good idea of all the parts that went together to drive a spark.

A very welcome letter arrived informing me that I had obtained a place in the party to ski on the BHP next winter, as had all of our Rover Crew who applied. This was good news and once again I would have to see the Apprentice Master Mr. Curtis to get permission for leave, but there was no hurry that could wait until I returned to Newport. In the first week of March I got a note that I was to return to work at Newport and report for duty in the erecting shop. I had enjoyed my time at the Jolimont Workshops and had learned a lot about the trains I travelled in every day, I also enjoyed working with the blokes I had worked with. Now I would have to get up earlier and wouldn't be able to go for a swim after work, but the days were shortening and it was no longer swimming weather. I said goodbye to all my mates and got ready on the Monday morning to get up early again to catch the 6.10 a.m. train.

CHAPTER 27

BACK AT NEWPORT THEN OFF TO SKI ON THE BHP 1948

I managed to catch the 6.10 a.m. train with the help of my loving mother, even though I told her again and again that I could get my own breakfast, but she would have none of it. One of the first jobs I had back at Newport was working with fitters on a K class helping to install the heavy motion gear, the coupling and connecting rods on the locomotive, which was no easy task, but very satisfying seeing it all go together. The hours were now shorter with the 40 hour week, the same as there had been at Jolimont. A strange thing happened, because we were told that apprentices would have to work on Fridays for another forty five minutes after the rest of the blokes in the erecting shop went home. Why I wondered? But I never really worked it out, although I believed it had something to do with the fact that apprentices were not covered by the full 40 hour week agreement.

Fitters installing the motion gear on a K class
Photo VRBTRS

Be that as it may, each Friday turned out to be a bit of a farce. There was one Senior Foreman left to supervise those of us who were supposed to have been left on work for forty five minutes that needed no supervision. I can remember one Friday when an apprentice who had a legitimate job on the top of the boiler of a locomotive, and who from his high vantage point could see where the Senior Foreman was wandering around, would indicate this to us and we moved around to where the foreman couldn't see us and it all resulted in a game of hide and seek! It was hilarious and served no purpose. When I returned to Newport I went to see Mr. Curtis to get permission to take two weeks off to go skiing. This time I was told that yes, I could take the two weeks holiday, but that would be the last time that leave other than at Christmas. Harry Gilham said when he went to get permission, he got the same response.

Back at the erecting shop I quickly came to the realization that I was no longer the smallest apprentice in the workshop. I had grown to become a quite a robust sort of young fellow and was no longer called on to fit into small places. I wondered if there were any small apprentices who were called on to do the jobs that I had been asked to do. I was however, never really aware of coming in contact with any other first year apprentices at all, our paths never seemed to cross, nor did I go again to have a 'sticky beak' in the brake shop to see how the new batch of first year apprentices were getting on with their cubes.

The 40 hour week and knocking off at 4.30 p.m., besides giving me a little more time with my mother and brothers also meant that every now and again I would meet my father on Princess Bridge station and ride home with him to Rosanna, of course in first class with all the other business type passengers, both men and ladies. There were days when I had been working on very dirty jobs and because the washing facilities in the erecting shop were not very good, although I did have clean hands and clean clothes, my face would be rather grimy. My father never seemed to be embarrassed talking with me as we travelled home, nor did he ever tell me that I should clean my face before I left work. He was a wonderful father, the best.

The months went by as I worked in the erecting shop enjoying the work and being back with my two mates Kevin and Allan. I was learning a lot more about locomotives working on a variety of classes. H 220 *Heavy Harry* came in for an overhaul, but this time I did not work on it. However an interesting event occurred during its overhaul. H 220 had just been lifted on high when the power to the two cranes was shut off and it hung there nearly all day until the power was restored. Winter was approaching and I was getting everything ready for my skiing holiday. Very soon I said goodbye to my workmates, that is, after I had spent the extra forty five minutes on Friday doing virtually nothing until it was time to knock off.

At last I was on the way to my skiing holiday on the BHP. The first snow falls of 1948 did not arrive as early as in previous years with the result that I only went once to Mt Donna Buang with the Rover Scouts. The ski run had only enough snow cover to be skiable and I must admit that after skiing on the BHP last year, skiing at Donna Buang was hardly worth the effort, especially as the weather was not too good either.

On Saturday morning 6th August 1948 I met the members of our party of Rovers Scouts and we boarded the train to take us to Bairnsdale, as usual hauled by a trusty A^2 locomotive. Even though I had been on this journey last year it was still exciting especially as I had with me so many members of my own crew. The train sped along through Moe, Warragul and Traralgon, but this time there was no change of locomotive at Sale as last year, the A^2 took us all the way to Bairnsdale, where we changed into the coach to take us to Omeo. I had made sure I had a map with me so I could follow the route our coach took, as well as being able to identify places of interest along the road as we went. The coach left Bairnsdale along the same road as last year and we arrived at the aptly named Hilltop Hotel. After a refreshing hot shower and a large meal we retired for the night to our rooms where I was soon fast asleep. The next morning after a hearty breakfast, we had a quick look around the township of Omeo with its charming, old style shops and houses. We then walked back up the steep hill to the Hilltop Hotel to board our coach to take us to Fitzgerald's property at Shannon Vale. We stopped at the Angler's Rest Hotel for a short time while Bill Waters made arrangements for our meal on the return journey, before continuing on towards Fitzgerald's.

I told some of our Rover Crew that last year the coach had to back up to get around some of the corners, but they didn't believe me because it didn't happen this time. However, sometime later while discussing the coach ride from Omeo, a Rover from another Crew who had been in our party last year, told our disbelieving Rovers that what I had told them was certainly true. Maybe the road had been widened on those curves or we had a better driver. It didn't matter whatever the reason was, because my story had been confirmed Arriving at Fitzgerald's homestead sometime before noon on Sunday morning, the same great welcome as last year was given to Bill Waters by the Fitzgerald's. We took our rucksacks and skis off the coach and they were loaded on the packhorses by Tom and Bren Fitzgerald.

****

One night after dinner I was talking to Bob Phillips a Rover from the Camberwell Crew. I told Bob that sadly this would be the last time I would be coming to the Chalet to ski, as I would not be given leave again during the winter. Bob thought for a moment and said: "Don't worry come and join the Youth Hostels Association and you can ski on Mt Buller with YHA on weekends." Bob said he was a member and 'club night' was held each Monday night in rooms in

Flinders Lane. He said. "Come to club night and he would introduce me to the members" I said I certainly would. I was very pleased with his suggestion as it seemed I would still be able to ski in the winter. I thought of the old saying; 'When one door closes, another door opens.' Unbeknown to me at that moment this was a really a *very, big door,* because it opened up my life to wonderful surprises and experiences that I am still relishing the benefits of to this day.

At the end of those two weeks at the Chalet, I had now spent a total of one month on the BHP in winter, coupled with the experience of hiking across the BHP on two occasions in the summer, I felt that I had an extremely good knowledge of the wonderful, unique, high alpine country of the Bogong High Plains, which had some wonderful significance for me in later years.

CHAPTER 28

I JOIN YHA – DISAPPOINTING NEWS AND SIGHTS 1948

I arrived back at work with not such a sun tanned face as I had last winter and it was good to get back to work on a locomotive with the same fitter that I had before my holiday. This time I was working on an N class, a locomotive that I had not had much to do with or seen many on the rails. I thought they looked a little ungainly. Such a long locomotive with a small diameter boiler above its 'Mikado' 2-8-2 wheel arrangement and motion gear with daylight being able to be seen between the two. The N was in for the overhaul of its motion gear, cylinder and valve pistons together with other minor parts. We removed the motion gear, slide bars, crossheads, valve and cylinder pistons and it was quite a revelation to see the large, 20 inch diameter, cylinder pistons come out of their cylinders. To me there did not seem to be anything wrong with them, however they were taken away to be overhauled. It was all very heavy work with much assistance from other fitters and the small overhead cranes. One of my main jobs after helping to remove the motion gear was using a die nut to clean up all the threads of the studs on the cylinders. A die nut is a nut with hardened, cutting teeth, the exact profile of the thread. They are made in all sizes and types of thread.

An N class 2-8-2

The nut is screwed all the way along the thread with a spanner and in so doing removes any dirt, scale or rust, together with repairing any minor damage to the thread. This was quite a long job, which I continued doing during the 45 extra minutes on Fridays when all the others had gone home.

A die nut

After I returned from the skiing, I was interested in seeing what the Youth Hostels Association (YHA) was all about, so I went into the YHA club night where we met Bob Phillips. He introduced me to the secretary and a few of his friends. The room was a hive of activity with girls and blokes all about my age talking together. They all seemed to be having a good time, as well as being very friendly. This was something new for me, being in the company of girls of my age, other than meeting them only at dances and Bible classes. I managed to learn a little about the Association's aims from a brochure I obtained that night and it seemed a good association to join.

Although my main aim of joining YHA for me was to go skiing at Mt Buller, but this was booked out for the season. However, skiing was only one of the many activities that YHA organisd. More such were hikes, bike rides, dances and other social occasions. It all seemed very interesting, so I decided to join then and there, even though I missed out skiing on Mt Buller. I left club night as a member of YHA, looking forward to joining in some of the activities in the near future, as well as going to club night again next Monday night. The club only had a small hostel on Mt Buller, but there were plans to build a new hostel in the future.

I was now 21 years of age and had the 'key of the door,' after having a very pleasant teetotal birthday party with my family and relatives, I had changed my appearance by growing a moustache and I began to smoke. So much of our fashions and lives, mine anyhow, were influenced by what we saw on the movies. I may have been 21, but I was still not a tradesman and this rankled a bit, however I soon got over that because life was so busy, so busy in fact that I stopped going to the VMRS. I had enjoyed being a member, but with YHA club nights each Monday night I could not fit it in and had lost interest. Model railways for me with the help of my father had been a wonderful hobby, but I had lost interest in that too.

Four months to go and then I would be a tradesman that was the thought that was going through my mind as the end of the year drew near. I was working in the erecting shop virtually without supervision, as I was competent to work on my own doing most tasks required of me on the N class and other locomotives I worked on in those last months. One day I received a memo from the Apprentice Master Mr. Curtis informing me that because I had been unable to get to work at Newport from my home in Rosanna when the strikes shut down the railways on many occasions; I would have to make up the time lost, to complete my apprenticeship. The time lost was a one day strike in 1945, a one day and a nine day strike in 1946, twenty four days in 1947, and three one day strikes in 1947-48, making a total of 38 days. The memo informed me that I would have to work on as an apprentice for an extra 38 days into 1949, before I completed my five-year apprenticeship and received my tradesman's fitter and turner certificate.

This was a huge disappointment quite apart from delaying the day I could call myself a fitter and turner without the word *apprentice* prefix. It also meant that I would have to wait to get a full tradesman's wage of about £6 odd. I checked with Alan and Kevin to see how they fared. Allan too because he couldn't get to work by train from Sandringham had to serve the same extra number of days as me. Kevin lived in Newport and walked to work and as there were a few strike days when the railways stopped, but not the tradesmen in the workshops, Kevin was able to work, so his extra days were a few short of we two. However we consoled each other and looked forward to early 1949 when we would in fact become tradesman. Harry Gilham my coppersmith apprentice friend, also had to serve the same extra time as myself.

One day in the erecting shop I was confronted with a sight that made me very disappointed and sad. An S class locomotive, I can't remember which one, came in for some sort of overhaul. The whole locomotive was very dirty, the streamline panels, the motion gear, wheels, together with the beautiful, blue, and gold lined streamlining panels all needed a thorough cleaning and painting to bring them back to their former glory. That of course was not to speak of any mechanical overhauling and repair work that needed to be carried out. I did not see the streamline paneling being taken off the s class, and stored, because I was still working on the N class down the far end of the erecting shop.

The next time I walked up to have a look at the S class, perhaps a couple of days later, I was further saddened and disappointed by the scene that unfolded before my eyes. The side panels that had been removed were lying on the floor of the workshop beside the locomotive. That was not the only indignity to Australia's famous locomotive. The next time I had a look, because the panels took up most of the space between another locomotive on the adjacent rails, the panels were still there and being walked on and over. Sacrilege! In the first year of my apprenticeship, I saw how all the streamlining panels under Orb's guidance when they were taken off the S class, were wrapped in thick hessian before the crane lifted them with rope slings and took them across the other side of the erecting shop to be safely stored away from damage. The next time I went and had a look they had been removed, but where to I wasn't sure. It was a pity that during the first five years of my apprenticeship the pride in the iconic *Spirit* locomotive (and maybe the whole train) had deteriorated to the condition and care that I witnessed.

There were only four S class locomotives to share the load of hauling the *Spirit of Progress* to Albury and back every day a task they carried out superbly with very few problems. On rare occasions when no S Class was available, H 220 hauled the *Spirit of Progress,* and although H 220 did not have the same allowable, top speed, of 70 mph (110 km/h) as the S class locomotives, it managed to keep the schedule because it was not slowed down on the steep climb over the Great Dividing Range. The men who fired the S class on the 3 hours 50 minutes journey both ways between Melbourne and Albury must have been very fit and dedicated firemen, because the locomotive's coal consumption was around 4,200lb (1.950 kg) per hour. This required the fireman to shovel coal into the firebox at the rate of seven shovels each minute, a huge task. I wonder if he had a tea break during the journey as I would think union rules required.

One day just after lunch I had an accident when I jammed my thumb between two pieces of metal and it hurt like hell. I had to go to the medical centre to have the blood drained from beneath my finger nail. The nurse used a red hot needle to burn through the nail to release the blood, which oozed out and in so doing relieved some of the pain. She gave me a pain killer and said that I would have to go on light duties for a couple of days. On those very rare occasions when I hurt myself such that I was not able to perform normal work like this day, I was put on 'light duties.' This might be carrying out a number of tasks such as sorting paper work, running messages around the workshops and various other small jobs. One of the duties I was asked to do this time was to deliver packages of files to Head Office in Spencer Street and because it was in the afternoon, and there was nothing I had to take back to Newport I was told I could go straight home. The light duties were allocated to employees on light duty by a clerk in the clock tower and after two days I was allowed to go back to work, albeit with a black, but not sore thumb. There were other occasions when I got a piece of steel in my eye and it could not be removed by the nurse at the medical centre at the workshops, I was sent with a bandage over my eye on the train to the Queen Victoria hospital to have it removed under a local anesthetic.

There were also other reasons when a trip up to the Queen Victoria Hospital gave me a diversion from time in the workshops. I think that it was in the third year of our apprenticeships that Kevin, Allan and I were approached and asked if we would like to give blood to the Red Cross Blood Bank. We all agreed and on different days, and twice each year thereafter we would be given time off to take the train up to the city and go to the Queen Victoria Hospital where I would lie down and have the blood taken. Afterwards I would be given a cup of coffee or tea and a biscuit and made to lie down for 30 minutes before I was allowed to leave and. if it was in the afternoon, I went home.

Walking out to the front of the erecting shop one afternoon past the S class, which was still in the throes of its overhaul I talked to a fitter who, together with a boilermaker and a labourer were dismantling an X class getting it ready for a thorough overhaul. The X class was a sad sight, stripped to its underwear, its boiler cladding, motion gear, compressor, smoke deflectors and piping were all gone, with some of the bits lying on the ground beside it looking like a pile of scrap metal. December 1948 was fast approaching and I was wondering where I would be working over the Christmas holidays. Everyone in the erecting shop I asked said

The X class outside the workshop

that they would be taking their holidays at Christmas, so I didn't think I would be still working in the erecting shop. I thought I might ask the Apprentice Master if I could go and work at Jolimont again, but thought better of it. However, I soon got my answer when I was told by the Senior Forman that I would be working in the turnery and I was to report there the day after Boxing Day, so that was settled. I knocked off for the Christmas holidays on Friday afternoon Christmas Eve. But for the strikes this would have been the day I received my Turner and Fitter's Tradesman's Certificate.

With my family I had a happy Christmas day and Christmas Dinner, with a succulent roast of lamb cooked by my mother. Because Christmas and Boxing Days were on Saturday and Sunday I did not return to the workshops and the turnery until Tuesday. When I reported to the foreman I found that I would be with a small group of fitters and turners and a labourer. Our job was to go round to all the various machines, checking and replacing belts and pulleys, greasing and lubricating, replacing cutting fluid and hydraulic oil reservoirs in machines such as the Blohm grinders and milling machines, while the labourer assisted us with the removal of swarf from machines and generally gave them a clean up. I enjoyed this work, which was interesting and fairly clean. I got to see a lot of machines that I had never seen before, mainly different types of lathes. I also became acquainted with the fluids, lubricating, cutting and hydraulic oils used by each machine. 1948 came to an end when I knocked off on New Year's Eve, wished the blokes a happy new year and headed off home. More of significance, was the fact in 1949 I was now beginning the fifth year of my apprenticeship.

CHAPTER 29

SERVING THE EXTRA 38 DAYS TO BE A TRADESMAN 1949

On Australia Day weekend in the new year of 1949 I went surfing with YHA to Lorne sleeping in my hike tent, and that was really a new experience in many ways. Of course being with young lady members was so different from the all male Rover Scouts, and I soon had my first girl friend. Since I joined YHA I had only gone to a couple of Rover Scout meetings just to keep in touch.

I began work back at Newport in 1949 the fifth year of my apprenticeship all because of the strikes, but in retrospect I reckon it was worth it to gain the shorter working week. The maintenance work in the turnery came to an end when the holidays ended, and I returned to work in the erecting shop as I had been instructed. I didn't miss not going to the Olympic Pool when I worked at Jolimont, because on a couple of especially hot days, I took the train a couple of stations further on from Newport to Williamstown Beach where I sun bathed and swam before returning home. Williamston beach was a nice beach with clean sand and water, quite comparable to the beach conditions I was used to at Edithvale.

The S class was gradually being put together, but the next time I went to have a look, it was gone. I like to think that its paint work was in a condition that still reflected the train's reputation as being the 'Pride of the VR', like it was when I first saw it in the first week of my apprenticeship. Seen speeding along from a distance where the imperfections were probably not that visible, the *Spirit of Progress* would still have provided a most impressive and awe inspiring sight, as it did in the dusk on the way home from the Rover Scout work party. As I write this however, I have no recollection at all of trying to see there were lights under the panels that lit up the motion gear so well on that occasion, or of asking Orb about it, but I know what I saw. How could I have forgotten to find out about that I do not know? On second thoughts I don't remember seeing Orb around the S class when I witnessed the uncaring manner in which the streamlining was treated when it had been dismantled. Maybe he was on holiday, or perhaps disgusted, resigned or asked to be given a different job in the workshops.

I worked on various locomotives with various fitters during the last extra days of my apprenticeship and while all of this was keeping me occupied, I was counting down the days when I would become a fully-fledged tradesman. Allowing for public holidays, I reckoned that the 38 days I still had to serve until I would at last become a tradesman, would be up on Wednesday February 16th 1949. Allan, Kevin and I were all working under the big saw tooth roof of the erecting shop, and we spent many lunch hours together talking. I told them about YHA, but neither seemed very interested. It would be good not to have to spend the 45 minutes extra mucking around on Fridays when all the rest had gone home.

And so the days went by as January 1949 came to an end and it was February, the month when I would have *served my time*, a common term used to describe our apprenticeship, not time in jail, which is what some thought I meant when I used the term.

CHAPTER 30

I QUALIFY TO BE TRADESMAN FITTER AND TURNER

On Wednesday February 16th 1949 I should have received some notification on this day I was now a Tradesman Fitter and Turner, but sadly, I have no recollection of anything out of the ordinary happening on that very important day in my working life. Wednesday 16th February 1949 was when I calculated after serving the extra 38 days. Besides the other memos I had received from the Apprentice Master during my apprenticeship, the last memo that I could remember receiving was that very disappointing one, informing me that I had to serve another 38 days before of my apprenticeship was completed. I am sure I would have remembered receiving a memo congratulating me on completing my apprenticeship as a fitter and turner and some indication about the presentation of my tradesman's certificate.

I would have thought too that I would have received a note from the paymaster that my wage would be increased to the full tradesman's rate the next pay day, but sadly I have also no recollection of being informed of that either. I am sure I did receive my tradesman's certificate, but how I do not know. I certainly do remember proudly showing it to my parents and brothers, so I must have received it somehow. Two of my friends Harry Gilham and Wal Stevens, who served his apprenticeship at Newport and North Melbourne, but ten years after me, also do not recall any details about the completion of their apprenticeship and the manner in which they obtained their trade certificate.

After a time lapse of sixty years, I was happily able to have telephone contact with Kevin and we had many long talks on the phone about the time we were at Newport. Kevin also has no memory of the day he became a tradesman and how he received his trade certificate. We were not able to establish contact with Allan Henderson

I left the Newport Workshops elated to be a tradesman, but very disappointed at the complete lack of any form of congratulations from the Apprentice Master Mr. Curtis in receiving my Tradesman's Certificate, especially as the wonderful manner in which Mr. Curtis had faultlessly organized and looked after us during the five years of our apprenticeships, and I would have liked to have shaken his hand and thanked him for his care..

I really knew I was a tradesman fitter and turner when I received my first pay packet sometime after Wednesday 16th, which contained my first, tradesman's weekly award wage of around £7, and I was able to knock off on Fridays at the same time as all the other tradesmen. So ended a wonderful five years of *LEARNING A TRADE,* which was to provide me with a very exciting and wonderful life.

Very soon after I became a tradesman, I joined the Amalgamated Engineering Union (AEU) the metal trades union that all fitters and turners in the VR belonged to. I was a member of the union until 1981 when I was appointed to the salaried position of Facilities Engineer at Australian General Electric Housewares in Notting Hill Victoria, where I worked for eighteen years until the company closed down in 1983.

AFTERWARDS

As I write this on the 28th May 2025 on the 19th May I turned 98 years of age, and I have every expectation of reaching 100 years, as I am still in reasonable health. I have written about my wonderful life after I left the VR in various unpublished and published books that are available on the internet under my name. The original book *Learning a Trade* was never published, but I sold many copies at apprentice reunions over the years and at model railway shops.

I was invited to join a party of YHA members who were going to spend a week skiing on Victoria's highest mountain Mt. Bogong 6,5008 ft. and staying at the Cleve Cole Memorial Lodge. Soon after one of the YH members Leon Langley approached me and asked me if I would like to join him to sail to the UK and work and backpack for about two years. I did not know Leon well, but my girlfriend Judy, another YHA member who I was in love with and she with me suddenly, without much warning she sailed away to the UK. This set off a train of thought, and after a lot of decision making I decided to follow her.

It so happened that another member of YHA had been enticing me to leave the VR and work for him at my trade and make a lot of money. This answered the big question of where would I get the money to pay for this adventure. So I resigned from the VR because they would not give me two years leave. The rest is history, about which I have written in many books some of which have been published by Tale Publishing and are listed below.

Come on Board   All about my voyage to England on the *Moreton Bay* and return form Naples to Port Melbourne on the *Orion*.

An Aussie Backpacking Londoner   All about living, and working at my trade in London for twelve months and the Coronation of Queen Elizabeth II.

Backpacking By Train   Describes five backpacking tours through England, Scotland, Norway, Sweden, Denmark, Germany, Austria, Switzerland, Italy and France,

Fitters working on an X class in the erecting shop at Newport
Drawing by Robert Emerson Curtis

Courtesy of Arthur Spartalis Fine Art Subiaco

ABOUT THE AUTHOR

The author 24 years

Gordon James Robert Smith. Author, historian and artist was born in 1927 in Victoria. He went to the Heidelberg State School and the Preston Technical School, and became a tradesman fitter and turner with the Victorian Railways (VR) in 1949. He was a member of the Cubs, Boy Scouts, Rover Scouts and the Youth Hostels Association (YHA). Together with another YHA member he left Australia in 1951 to travel by ship to the UK on a working and backpacking holiday for two years. He returned to Australia in 1953. Soon after, in December 1953, he joined the SEC Kiewa Hydro-Electric Scheme and began water colouring. In 1954 he married Dilys Terry and during his ten years on the Scheme, they raised a family of a girl and two boys. In 1963 he and his family left the SEC and shifted to Melbourne where he worked for Australian General Electric (AGE) as a facilities engineer until AGE closed down in 1983. He then taught pneumatic and hydraulics at the Royal Melbourne Technical College (RMIT) until he retired in 1993. He played golf and skied for much of his life. After he retired he began writing many books about his life. He is now 98 and lives with his wife, also 98 in Box Hill North.

The author 94 years

BOOKS BY THE AUTHOR

Co-authored Pneumatic Control for Industrial Automation, published by John Wily. *Come on Board,* and *An Aussie Backpacking Londoner* both published by Tale.: Self published-*An Australian Backpacker Abroad 1951-1953-Mountains of My Youth-Working and Raising a Family On The Kiewa Scheme* and *Learning a Trade 1944 to 1949-20 Watercolours of the Kiewa Scheme.* He has published the following Ebooks on Smashwords. *Two Voyages-My Journey Through Occupied Austria 1952-To the Swiss Alps via Venice-The Assimilation Of An Aussie Backpacker-Backpacking in 1952-An Aussie Backpacking Londoner-Back to Australia via France and Italy-Concrete Hard Rock Earth and Snow-The High Plains Patrol.* His last two were *Backpacking by Train* and *Skiing In Zermatt 1952.*

www.ingramcontent.com/pod-product-compliance
Lightning Source LLC
Chambersburg PA
CBHW042317090526
44583CB00024BA/3024